The Seer

by Ali Smith

First performed at the Spectrum Centre, Inverness on 3 May 2006

Scottish Tour 3 May – 17 June 2006

Originally commissioned by the Highland Festival

**Highlands & Islands
ENTERPRISE**

Scottish
Arts Council
LOTTERY FUNDED

The Seer

by Ali Smith

VIVIEN GRAHAME	**Iona**
DOUGLAS RUSSELL	**Neil**
SARAH HAWORTH	**Kirsty**
IRENE ALLAN	**Sabrina**
MAIRI MORRISON	**Janice/Mrs Henderson**

Director	Matthew Zajac
Set Designer	David Ramsay
Costume Designer	Kirsteen Naismith
Lighting Designer	Cara Wiseman
Sound Designer	Andy Thorburn
Production Manager	David Ramsay
Stage Manager	Cara Wiseman
Producers	Matthew Zajac
	Hamish MacDonald
Administrator	Lara McDonald
Publicity Design	Karen Sutherland
Publicity Photographer	Laurence Winram
Press	Catherine Bromley
	(07843 626042)

Biographies

Vivien Grahame *Iona*

Vivien trained in acting at RSAMD in Glasgow and is also a stand-up comedian and performance poet. Her recent theatre appearances include *Wee Witches* for Lickety Spit and *Metagama* for Theatre Hebrides. Television credits include *Revolver, Velvet Soup* and *The Stand-Up Show* for the BBC. Later this year she appears in a film called *Voodoophone* and last year she played the title role in the award winning short film *The Most Boring Woman in the World*.

Douglas Russell *Neil*

Aberdonian Doug studied mediaeval history at St. Andrews University and Film and Theatre at Emory University, Atlanta, Georgia, USA. Recent theatre includes: *Othello, Julius Caesar, Sleeping Beauty, The Princess and the Goblin* (Royal Lyceum, Edinburgh), *Sunset Song, Romeo and Juliet* (Prime Productions), *The Beauty Queen of Leenane, King of the Fields* (Mull Theatre), *Aladdin, Peter Pan* (Eden Court Theatre, Inverness). TV: *Rebus, Taggart, High Road* (STV), *Battlefield Britain, Culloden, Zig Zag, The Vikings* (BBC), *The Red Fox, The Real Tartan Army* (Caledonia, Sterne & Wyld) and *Low Winter Sun* (Tiger aspect for Channel 4). Doug lives in Edinburgh with his beautiful Dundonian wife Larissa and two ungrateful cats, Maisie and Dusty, who like killing things.

Sarah Haworth *Kirsty*

Sarah hails from the stoney shores of Stornoway but moved to 'The Mainland' when she was knee high to a squirrel's thigh. She trained at Queen Margaret University College in Edinburgh. Theatre roles include The Herald in *Marat/Sade*, Germaine in *The Guid Sisters*,   Rose in *Dancing at Lughnasa* and Baby Gumboyle in *Dr Dog*. She appears in the upcoming feature film *Red Road*. Sarah is delighted to be playing the part of Kirsty and believes the play is the most innovative, eloquent and advanced she has ever read.

Irene Allan   *Sabrina*

Irene Allan trained at Queen Margaret College, Edinburgh. Her theatre work includes: *The Memorandum* and *Zlata's Diary* (Communicado); *Treasure Island* (Belgrade Theatre, Coventry); *The Prime Of Miss Jean Brodie* (Royal National Theatre); *Chopin In Midcalder* (Theatre Objektiv); *The Prime Of Miss Jean Brodie, Phaedra, Peter Pan, Macbeth, Sleeping Beauty and The Merchant Of Venice* (Lyceum, Edinburgh); *Oleanna* (Theatre Informer); *A Christmas Carol* and *Bondagers* (Byre Theatre); *Puddock and the Princess* (Scottish Actors' Initiative); *Tamlane* (Theatre Alba); *Hildegarde* (Firstbase). Her radio and film works include: *For The Love Of Willie* (BBC Radio 4), *Tollcross Tales* and *Baby Boom or Bust* (Pepperhouse Productions).

Mairi Morrison   *Janice/Mrs. Henderson*

Mairi Morrison graduated from the RSAMD with an MDra in Acting. She is also a professional singer and presenter. Her first appearance at the Edinburgh Festival was with her self-penned one-woman show *Beasts of Holm*. Other theatre credits include: *The Sked Crew* & *Metagama* (Theatre Hebrides); *Cupa Ti is Pios* (Really Skint Theatre Co.); *A Chraobh is Airde* & *Seumas* & *na Lochlannaich* (TOSG Theatre Co.); *Journey* (Dance House/Unam Choir). TV & Film include: *Bad Brown Owl* (BBC/Comedy Unit); *The Iolaire* (Rapid Eye Productions); *Taggart* (STV); *Gruth is Uachdar* (BBC); *An Roghainn* & *Miulaigh* (Studio Alba); *Ceolraidh* (MNE); *Carlas* (SMG); various voiceover credits. Mairi has appeared on numerous music programmes and has written and performed music for various BBC children's programmes. She regularly tutors in drama and is currently commissioned to write and direct a community play in Tiree.

Ali Smith   *Writer*

Ali Smith was born in Inverness and lives in Cambridge. She's the author of 6 books, the most recent being *The Whole Story and Other Stories* (2004) and *The Accidental* (2005).

Matthew Zajac *Director/Producer*

Born in Inverness, Matthew studied Drama at Bristol University. He has worked as an actor for over 20 years, appearing in numerous productions in all media throughout the UK. He was a founder member of the London-based theatre company Plain Clothes Productions, producing, acting and directing for the company's six productions. These included *Blue Night in the Heart of the West* (Bush Theatre, winner of the George Devine Award), *Wolf* (Traverse/ Young Vic) & *Her Sister's Tongue* (Lyric Studio Hammersmith). As Associate Director of Grey Coast Theatre Company, he directed the Helmsdale Community play *The Great Bunillidh Volcano & Camster*. He has also directed for the popular children's company Licketyspit. Matthew has produced two films, *The Beauty of the Common Tool* (1st Prize, Palm Springs International Short Film Festival) and the digital feature *Gordon Bennett*, in which he also takes the title role. Recent work includes Mr. Hansen in *Further Than the Furthest Thing* (Prime Productions/Byre Theatre), Creon in *Antigone* (TAG), Joe Saul in *Burning Bright* (N.amp), Long Rob in *Sunset Song* (Prime Productions), Boris in *Karl Marx's Beard* (Theatre Objektiv), *Dr. Korczak's Example* (BBC Radio 4), all the male roles in *Seven Ages* (Dogstar) and screen appearances in *The Planman, Low Winter Sun* and the feature films *Young Adam* and *Man To Man*. Matthew is Joint Artistic Director of Dogstar Theatre with Hamish Macdonald.

David Ramsay *Set Designer/Production Manager*

This is David's third Highlands and Islands tour with Dogstar Theatre Company, fulfilling the roles of Production Manager and Set Designer.

Originally From Dallas in Morayshire, he now lives in Glasgow working in television and film. Covering a multiplicity of roles, David always works within the areas of set, props, design and construction. TV and film includes: *An Anarchist's Story* (Pelicula Films), *Contorted Hazel* (Mandragora Productions), *High Times* (series 2 3MG), *Comedy Gold* (MNE/The Comedy Unit), *Dud Brown Owl* (The Comedy Unit), *Gamerz* (Pure Magic Films), *Baldy McBane* (Nobles Gate Films). Theatre includes: *The Strathspey King, Seven Ages* (Dogstar), *Brazil 12 Scotland 0* (Birds of Paradise), *King Lear* (Bard in the Botanics), *The Story Nation* (Dumfries and Galloway Arts Association), *Cinderella* (Team Entertainments), *The Jasmine Road, Saame Sita, I Have Before Me, Adventures in a Bath* (Theatre Workshop), *Cry Out* (Out of The Darkness Theatre Co), *The Big Shop* (Edinburgh Puppet Company). Also the designer and maker of bespoke sculptural lighting known as 'Ramshackle Lamps'.

Kirsteen Naismith   Costume Designer

Kirsteen graduated from Cardonald College, Glasgow, where she studied Fashion and Clothing Technology. She has worked extensively in theatre and television as a Dresser, Wardrobe Assistant, Wardrobe & Costume Supervisor and, more recently, as a Costume Designer. Recent theatre credits include: *Perfect Pie* (Stellar Quines/Byre Theatre); *Further Than the Furthest Thing* (Prime Productions/Byre Theatre); *Heal* (Sounds of Progress). She has also toured with Scottish Opera, working on *The Death of Klinghoffer, La Boheme & The Ring Cycle* and has worked on countless pantomimes at the King's Theatre, Glasgow. TV includes: *People's Court, Heartless, Win, Lose or Draw, The Karen Dunbar Show, The House That God Built, Terri McIntyre, The Planman, Laugh Out Loud, Harry and the Wrinklies, Taggart, Wheel of Fortune.* Film: *Nina's Heavenly Delights, Gamerz, Can't Bank On Heaven, All Over Brazil.*

Cara Wiseman   *Lighting Designer/Stage Manager*

Cara's interest in lighting design began at a young age after helping with productions at school. She now works as a freelance technician around Scotland. Lighting Designs to date include: *Aladdin* (Team Entertainments) *Passing Places, Romeo & Juliet* (Brunton Youth Theatre), *I Love You Numb, Such Is Nature* (National Tours with Cat In A Cup Theatre Company), *Emma's Child, Come Back to the Five & Dime Jimmy Dean* (Gateway Theatre). She regularly works as a relight technician and wishes to carry on working in the touring theatre industry.

Andy Thorburn   Sound Designer

Andy Thorburn has composed and compiled theatre music for more than 20 productions in as many years with Eden Court Theatre, Inverness, Grey Coast Theatre, Theatre Highland and Right Lines as well as companies in Edinburgh and Glasgow. He has toured worldwide as a piano and keyboard player with the successful *Blazin' Fiddles, Mouth Music* and the exotic *Loveboat Orchestra*. The exciting medium of theatre soundscape allows him to write in many styles: 12-tone serialism; Scottish traditional folk; modern chamber music; and computer-based multitrack digital scores. He is also busy with teaching and tutor-training at school level and for the Royal Scottish Academy of Music and Drama.

Hamish MacDonald   *Producer*

Hamish MacDonald has experience in touring theatre in Scotland dating back to Faultline Cabaret's Thatcher era satirical comedy *The Kilt Is Our Demise*. He recently completed The Robert Burns Fellowship for the Dumfries and Galloway Arts Association, a writer's residency that included the commissioning and production of four new plays performed in 2005, *The Pilgrim's Tale, The Heretic's Tale, The Bard's Tale* and *The Scunner's Tale.* He has adapted two of his plays, *The Captain's Collection* and *The Strathspey King,* both Dogstar Theatre touring productions, into international award-winning series for BBC Radio Scotland. Further playwriting for Dogstar includes *Seven Ages* (toured Scotland 2004), and also *Slainte Mhath Mr Capone* for Highland Festival 2004. Hamish is author of the novel *The Gravy Star* (11:9 Publishing, 2001) and has written fiction and poetry for the award winning Scots language imprint Itchy Coo Publishing, including the teenage novella *The Girnin Gates* and several manky mingin rhymes in Scots in *King o the Midden* and *Blethertoun Braes.*

Karen Sutherland   *Publicity Design*

Graphic Designer, illustrator and artist living in the Highlands, Karen studied at Glasgow School of Art. She illustrated the award winning *Animal ABC, Eck the Bee, A Moose in the Hoose, Katie's Coo* and is currently working on *Katie's Moose,* all with Itchy Coo. Itchy Coo is a best-selling imprint which specialises in Scots language books for children and young people. Itchy Coo is a partnership between B&W Publishing and writers Matthew Fitt and James Robertson. www.itchy-coo.com

For

The Seer

Dogstar would like to thank

Timorous Beasties for their wonderful wallpaper

Patrick at Thrifty Car Rental

Comunn Nan Eilean Siar (W. Isles Council)

Islesburgh Trust, Shetland

Hi Arts Ltd.

Stewart Mackay, Lorzcom Ltd.

Kingsmills Scouts, Inverness

St. James Church, Leith

The Ramsay Family, Kim Macdonald, Grace McDonald,
Bruce MacGregor, Maggie Dunlop, Alyth MacCormack,
Alastair Macdonald, Mrs. Kay Burton, Anya McDonald,
Haesel McDonald

Craig Duncan, Anna Zajac, Virginia Radcliffe

The Seer

Scottish Tour May 3 – June 17 2006

MAY 3 & 4	Inverness – Spectrum Centre
5	Strathpeffer Pavilion
6	Isle of Skye – Sabhal Mòr Ostaig
9	Gorthleck – Stratherrick Hall
10	Lochinver VIllage Hall, Sutherland
11	Lyth Arts Centre, Caithness
12	Rosehall Village Hall, Sutherland
13	Glenmoriston Millennium Hall
16	Plockton Village Hall
17	Ullapool – MacPhail Theatre
18	Isle of Lewis, Stornoway – An Lanntair
19	Benbecula – St Mary's Hall
20	Barra – Castlebay Community School
23	Paisley Arts Centre
25	Aberdeen – The Lemon Tree
26	Aboyne – Deeside Theatre
27	Stirling – MacRobert Arts Centre
31	St John's Town of Dalry – High School
JUNE 2 & 3	Shetland – Garrison Theatre
7	St Andrews – Byre Theatre
8	Dunfermline – Carnegie Hall
9	Arbuthnott – Grassic Gibbon Centre
10	Newtonhill – Bettridge Centre
12	Isle of Mull – Dervaig Village Hall
13	Kilmelford & Kilninver Village Hall, Argyll
14	Livingston – Howden Park Centre
15	Kingussie – The Badenoch Centre
16 & 17	Edinburgh – Traverse Theatre

 **DOGSTAR** THEATRE **www.dogstartheatre.co.uk**

In recent years, Dogstar has established itself as one of the leading theatre companies from the Highlands of Scotland. We are based in Inverness, one of Europe's fastest growing small cities. Our productions tour throughout Scotland, but we especially serve our region and its people. Our work springs directly from the Highlands' defining characteristics: a stunningly beautiful and harsh natural landscape; a tumultuous and marginalised history; a shifting and changing population; a vibrant oral and musical tradition. Our productions endeavour to speak to our audiences in the Highlands and beyond using some of Scotland's best actors, musicians, writers, directors and designers. For us, theatre is a place for celebration and debate, for entertainment and ideas, for a few laughs, a few tears, a challenge to the mind and a memorable night out. At its heart, it's about communication between the actor and the audience. It can't exist without you.

Each of the company's productions to date has been written by Hamish MacDonald. *The Seer* represents a development of the company's work as we broaden our scope to include work by other writers.

Dogstar Theatre is a member of the Federation of Scottish Theatre and the Highlands & Islands Theatre Network.

Artistic Directors Hamish MacDonald & Matthew Zajac

Board Anne Macleod Catherine MacNeil Hugh Nicol Brian Spence

Dogstar Theatre
87, Cradlehall Park, Inverness IV2 5DB, Scotland

dogstartheatre@blueyonder.co.uk
www.dogstartheatre.co.uk

Productions

Redcoats, Turncoats & Petticoats (1998)

'. . . a deft blend of solid research, comic absurdity and withering satire . . . '

Inverness Courier

The Captain's Collection (1999 & 2000)

'Beautifully written . . . Lyrical and elegiac yet darkly reso-lute . . . Neither a homage nor a hatchet job – although it could have been either, it dwelt inside the psychological ruins of a complex, compromised and tortured Highlander . . .

The Scotsman

Seven Ages (2001 & 2004)

'. . . this eloquent show is a timely reminder of how much Scottish theatre needs this strand of Highland-made work with all its wild surrealism, structural anarchy, passionate lyricism and spiritual openness . . . '   *The Scotsman*

The Strathspey King (2003)

'. . . this was a piece of imaginative and beautifully realised music theatre honouring a flawed genius of Scottish music . . . '   *The Herald*

We are currently developing Henry Adam's *At the End of the World and In the Morning* (in conjunction with the National Theatre of Scotland), Matthew Zajac's *The Tailor of Inverness* and Hamish MacDonald's *The Heretic's Tale*.

Ali Smith
The Seer

faber and faber

First published in 2006
by Faber and Faber Limited
3 Queen Square, London WC1N 3AU

Typeset by Country Setting, Kingsdown, Kent CT14 8ES
Printed in England by Mackays of Chatham plc, Chatham, Kent

A CIP record for this book
is available from the British Library

ISBN 0–571–23445–3
ISBN 978–0–571–23445–5

2 4 6 8 10 9 7 5 3 1

Characters

Iona

Neil

Kirsty

Sabrina

Janice

Mrs Henderson

Act One

A trendier-than-thou Elle Decoration-*like living room
of a flat. Walls painted Edinburgh red, place scattered
with nice designer things – books, magazines, gadgets,
furniture. Two big armchairs, turned towards each other.
Front door to stage right, and another exit centre back.
Scottish-looking contemporary art and posters. Sixties-
design chair. Table, with cafetière still on it as if from
this morning's breakfast, and glasses and half a bottle
of wine as if from the night before. Clock on the wall
saying ten to six.*

*Music is playing as the audience comes in and settles
down. Old-fashioned, ceilidh-style music, tunes like
'Bluebell Polka', 'Dancing in Kyle', things the audience
will really recognise. This music carries on playing,
peculiarly and loud, after the lights have dimmed and
right into the start of the play . . .*

*Which begins when Iona enters, clearly just home from
work. She carries a briefcase, some bags. She opens the
front door, picks up the mail, kicks the door shut with
her foot, walks into the middle of the room, drops her
briefcase, etc., onto the floor, and shrugs her coat off,
letting it fall too.*

*She looks uneasily around her, as if wondering at the
music. Then she rips open the parcel in her hand, and
unpacks something, dropping the wrapping onto the
floor. It's a very fashionable salt-and-pepper grinder. She
looks at it, pleased.*

*But she can't help being distracted by the relentless
Scottish music.*

*She looks up again, worried, wondering where it's
coming from.*

5

She goes back to the front door, opens it and listens to see if the music's coming from out there. It's not. She closes the door, puzzled. She stands mid-stage again, looks blindly out towards the audience, seeing nothing, mystified, trying to see. She looks down. She gets down, puts her ear against the floor. She stands up, unsurely, unsurely stamps on the floor in case it's coming from down there.

The music goes on.

She goes over to the CD player, puts in a CD, turns it high, braces herself. Madonna blasts out, 'Material Girl'. She lets it blast for ten to fifteen seconds. Then she turns it right down, and listens.

Silence. The Scottish music has stopped. Iona looks immensely relieved.

Iona There.

She turns Madonna up a little, to a reasonable volume, takes off her cardigan, runs her hands through her hair – she's home at last. She sighs, leaves the cardigan on the back of one of the chairs and exits through the back.

Neil enters at the front door. He's home from work too. His briefcase is bigger than hers. He has a folded newspaper under his arm. He hangs his coat up neatly at the door. He sees Iona's coat and bags and the remainder of the postal wrapping all in the middle of the floor. He picks up her coat, smooths it down, hangs it up neatly with his. He picks up the salt-and-pepper grinder, appraises it. He decides he likes it. He tuts at Iona's cardigan on the chair (clearly it's his chair), picks it up, folds it, puts it on the other chair (hers). He puts the folded newspaper on his own chair. He goes to the CD player, ejects the Madonna CD, puts on one of his own. Travis, 'Why Does It Always Rain on Me?'

Enter Iona.

Iona Hello, love.

Neil Hello, love.

Iona What about my music?

Neil What about my music?

Iona Neil, I've been at work all day.

Neil Iona, I've been at work all day.

Iona Stop copying what I'm saying.

Neil I'm not copying what you're saying.

Iona You are.

Neil I'm not.

Iona I was listening to that.

Neil You weren't even in the room.

Iona I was still listening to it.

Neil Well, now I'm listening to this.

Iona I'm not wanting to listen to your noise.

Neil I'm not wanting to listen to *your* noise.

Iona You're doing it again.

Neil Doing what again?

Iona It.

Neil What?

Iona It.

Neil What?

Iona (*quietly, to herself, reining herself in*) Oh, for fuck sake.

Neil's face changes, as if he's incredibly shocked at her swearing.

Neil Is that the kind of language they speak at your work? Because it's not the kind of language I'm used to hearing in my home.

Iona gives in.

Iona Sorry. I'm sorry. It just slipped out.

Neil I hate it when women swear.

Iona Sorry.

Neil You know I do. It's so coarse.

Iona (*to mollify him*) Are you wanting some toast?

Neil No. (*mollified*) Maybe. What kind of bread is it?

Iona Um.

Neil Is it focaccia or ciabatta?

Iona Which is the one you like again?

Neil Iona, I can't eat ciabatta, you know that. It brings my mouth out in lumps. You know that.

Iona Yes, it's the . . . the other one. Do you want some?

Neil Do you want your coat to be wearable tomorrow or would you rather it was all creases when you went in to work?

Iona Eh? (*Looks at the floor where she left her coat. Looks at the coat rack.*) Oh. Thanks.

Neil Are these things on the floor for a reason?

Iona Yes, they're an art exhibition.

Neil What kind of an art exhibition? The art of leaving the flat in a state?

8

Iona What do you think of the new grinder? It came today.

Neil Quite nice, considering it was you that chose it.

Iona You're so horrible.

Neil Yes, but you like it that way.

Iona What are you wanting on your toast? Butter, jam or gruyère with basil?

Ncil Is toast all we're having for supper?

Iona (*going through to the back to make the toast*) No, I'm just making toast. I'm not making supper. It's not my turn to make the supper.

Neil It's not my turn to make the supper. (*He tucks her things under the table, then, satisfied that the room's tidy, pours himself a glass of wine.*) Mmm. (*He sits in his armchair, loosens his tie, opens his newspaper, sighs.*) What a day at work. (*louder*) What a day I had of it at work.

Iona (*coming back through, walking a little oddly, as if trying not to say out loud what she has to say*) Neil. Listen. I forgot to say. But that, eh, that music. It was playing again when I came in.

Neil (*wary, staying behind his newspaper*) Iona . . .

Iona (*furtive*) Not your music. I'm not getting at your music. I mean the Scottish music again. When I came in. It was playing really loud. It was definitely in here. I couldn't hear anything in the stairwell. Or anything outside. But when I came in here and shut the door, there it was again.

Neil Uh huh.

Iona I could hardly hear myself think.

Neil (*closing the newspaper, folding it deliberately*) Iona, that's enough.

Iona Then, just like before, I turned up Madonna really loud, and as usual when I turned it down again the other music had stopped.

Neil gets up wearily and goes over to the CD player, turning the sound off. Silence. He holds his hands up as if to say, 'Well, no music now.'

Iona I'm telling you, I bloody heard it, Neil.

Neil looks at her reproachfully. She backs down, but insists:

I *heard* it.

Neil Next it'll be seeing things.

Iona makes an exasperated sound. She exits through the back. Neil goes over to his golf clubs, standing in their bag up against a wall. Gets a putter out, and a ball. Carefully lines up the ball and the club, putts the ball across the room.

Iona (*from through the back*) You better not be hitting balls in there, Neil.

Neil ignores her, gets out another ball, lines it up carefully. Iona comes through.

Neil! The floor surfaces!

She takes the club out of his hands, holds a plate with toasted bread on it under his nose. He takes it. She sits down in her chair. He looks at the food on the plate.

Neil Iona. There's *basil* on this gruyère.

Iona You said you wanted basil.

Neil (*whine*) You know I hate basil. You know I can't eat anything with basil in it.

Iona Give it to me, I'll scrape it off.

Neil It's all melted *in*. It's melted into the cheese.

Iona It's only a little bit. It just fell on.

Neil It's not. It's right the way through the cheese. It's not like it's just on the surface. I can see it all under the top of it as well, really mixed in.

Iona But you didn't say you didn't want –

Neil I hate basil, love, you know that. There's nothing more horrible. I can't think of anything more hor—

Iona Oh for goodness sake.

Neil I can't believe you did that to my focaccia.

Iona It's just basil. It's nice.

Neil But basil makes the cheese taste really different. (*He sinks into his armchair, really deflated.*)

Iona (*getting up*) I'll make you more.

Neil No, it's okay. I don't want any now.

Iona I'll make it like you like it.

Neil No. I'm not hungry. You eat mine. I'll be fine. I'll just wait for supper. We should eat soon. I've a lot of work to do tonight.

Iona Me too.

Neil I've several case studies to look at.

Iona Me too.

Neil So . . . how many have you got?

Iona (*trying to outguess him*) I've . . . three.

Neil Ah. Because I've four.

Iona Yes, but I've an extra one and a half from the weekend that I wasn't counting in the original three, which actually makes four and a half.

Neil Yes, but they don't count.

Iona Yes, but they do count.

Neil They don't count.

Iona They do.

Neil Yes, but mine are really important.

Iona Mine are really important too.

Neil Yes, but my case studies are to do with the new Scotland. They're vital.

Iona So are mine. And it's your turn to make supper, Neil, and my turn to use the study.

Neil Yes. But I really need the study tonight.

Iona Oh, okay. Whatever. I'll work through here.

Neil And will you not play music while I'm working tonight while you're through here working? I really have a lot to do.

Iona Okay.

Neil I really have to get it done.

Iona Anyway, it'll give me a chance to phone my sister.

Neil Oh. Right. I thought you said you had a lot of work to do?

Iona I do. But I haven't spoken to Kirsty for ages. I haven't seen her for even longer. D'you know, it's been so long since I've seen her that if I were to see her again tonight I don't know if I'd know it was her?

Neil Do you think, if you phone her, you'll be on the phone for long tonight?

Iona Well, depends. Why?

Neil Oh, you know. In case anyone else is trying to phone.

Iona Like who?

Neil Well, work said they might phone.

Iona Tonight?

Neil They said they might.

Iona They've never phoned you at home before.

Neil Well, they said. They might. You're always on the phone for hours when you're on the phone to her.

Iona You're jealous.

Neil I'm not.

Iona You're jealous of anybody I speak to on the phone.

Neil I am not. I am not the jealous type. I'm not jealous of anything.

Iona And anyway. What if my work phones *me* while *your* work's on the phone?

Neil Your work never phones.

Iona They said they might phone.

Neil Tonight?

Iona Well, they said. They might.

Neil (*in the huff*) Maybe it's time we got our own phones. Maybe it's time we got separate phones.

Iona Yeah, maybe it is time we got separate phones.

They look at each other, dolefully. Then Iona, suddenly, as if remembering, says:

There's this Japanese girl at work, she's got a really nice one and it's only this big! I thought when I saw it, Neil'd really like that one, honestly, it's this big, that's all. (*Holds up her hand.*)

Neil Yeah, but folded out it'd be bigger than that. You can't get them that small. There wouldn't be room for any numbers.

Iona It is, Neil. That's the size of it. Literally. It is. I saw it. It's like the one in – wait a minute –

She reaches down the side of her armchair and picks up a magazine off the top of a pile, starts flicking through one, looking for something. Neil is now sitting in his chair, too. They're opposite each other, sitting in exactly the same position.

Neil So, is the Japanese girl at your work, like, really small?

Iona Eh, well, I suppose so. Not really. Well, she's not big.

Neil Japanese people maybe need really small phones because the size of their hands is smaller. Japanese people are really actually smaller than other types of people. They're one of the smallest nationalities in the world. (*He holds up his own hand and looks at it.*)

Iona Here. Look –

She holds the magazine, folded open, so Neil can see a picture of someone with a mobile.

Neil Actually, that is a really nice one.

Iona looks pleased.

How much?

Iona (*reading out*) 'Jumper wool, eighty-five pounds, Fenn Wright Manson. Trousers wool, one hundred pounds, John Lewis's. Sunglasses by Oliver Peoples, one hundred and seventy-seven pounds –' A hundred and seventy-seven pounds for sunglasses! 'Double duvet cover from the Calm range at House of Fraser . . .' Oh. It doesn't say about the phone.

Neil (*snatching the magazine*) Let me look. (*But he can't find it either.*) Oh.

Iona See?

Neil You always buy such stupid magazines.

Resentful silence ensues.

Iona Neil.

Neil What?

Iona Don't.

Neil What?

Iona Pick your nose.

Neil I wasn't.

Iona You were.

Silence again. They look at each other from their opposite armchairs with complete and comfortable liking and dislike.

Iona Do you really have to work tonight?

Neil Yes, but do you?

Iona Yes, but I could maybe put it off. I could do it tomorrow.

Neil I could do mine while you make the supper, and that would free me up, if you made the supper, for the rest of the evening.

Iona Or . . . *you* could make the supper and *I* could phone my sister.

Neil (*quick*) No you can't, because I told you, work might phone.

Iona You hate it, don't you?

Neil What?

Iona (*mimicking*) '*What?*' You hate it whenever I do anything that's nothing to do with you.

Neil That's not true.

Iona And you hate her.

Neil I don't.

Iona You hate my little sister.

Neil I don't.

Iona You do.

Neil I don't. It's just that she's so . . .

Iona What?

Neil Different.

Iona Different how?

Neil Just different. Just . . . not the same. Not like us.

Iona I remember when Kirsty and I were wee, and after our bath on a Saturday night our mother would –

Neil I know, I know, your mother would put you to bed, then Kirsty would lie next to you all night telling you all the stories, story after story, and you would both stay awake as long as you could and look at the stars and the moon and the morning coming up and all that stuff and everything.

Iona Well, there's no need to interrupt me.

Neil But that's exactly what I mean.

Iona What?

Neil Why do we always end up talking about Kirsty when we're about to have a nice night in just ourselves?

Iona It was you that brought her up.

Neil It was not. It was you.

Iona (*knowing it was*) It wasn't.

Neil Just when we're about to have a nice night in by ourselves. We've the whole evening stretching out like . . . like . . .

Iona Like all the other evenings?

Neil What'll we do? We could do anything. What'll we do?

Iona We could have sex.

Neil looks abashed.

Neil, you can't still be sore. That football injury's three years ago now.

Neil No, no, it's okay. We could have sex. I'd quite like to.

Iona No, no, it's okay. It was just, you know, an idea. I don't really want to.

They both look remarkably relieved.

We could, um . . .

Neil We could go out for a meal?

Iona Or we could go to the cinema.

Neil Or we could stay in and watch a video.

Iona Or we could do some online shopping.

Neil Or we could play on my PlayStation.

Iona Or we could read.

Neil Or we could . . . we could do anything.

Iona Yes.

Neil Yes. Every evening I give thanks, that our life together is so straightforward like this.

Iona Like there's no horrible drama in our lives, like the lives of couples you see on programmes on TV or in the papers.

Neil Yes, because neither of us is about to find out that we were adopted and didn't know it.

Iona Or abused and didn't know it, or about to have to have an abortion.

Neil Or an AIDS test.

Iona Or an affair.

Neil Nothing unsettling ever happens to us.

Iona Perfect.

Neil No drama ever happens to us.

Iona Thank goodness. Nothing.

Neil It's so nice, to be so absolutely sure of who we are and where we are in the world.

Iona Nothing left to question. Bliss.

Neil So – what'll we do tonight?

Iona We could do something.

Neil We could. Or –

Iona We could do nothing.

Neil We could. We could do nothing.

They settle back smugly into their armchairs, to spend the whole evening luxuriously doing nothing. But just at the moment they've both settled –

There's a loud knock on the door.

Complete shock on both their faces. It's the first time in the play (apart from when Iona heard the music at the beginning, or tried to talk to Neil about it) that they've looked at all alive or unsettled. They stare at each other, amazed, unable to speak even.

There's a knock again. Louder, even more demanding. Now when they speak to each other it's with a new sharpness. Whereas all evening they've acted with each other as if they've always known exactly what the other was going to say, now everything is edgy, as if they have absolutely no idea what's coming next. This next conversation is in hushed tones.

Neil Did you –

Iona Uh –

Neil Did you hear –

Iona Yes. Did you –

Neil We're not expecting –

Iona No, no, I'm not –

Neil Well who's this, then?

Iona How would I know? Do you know?

Neil No, I don't –

Iona It's never happened –

Neil What'll we –

Louder knocking. They look at each other, in terror.
The door bursts open. A big, really scruffy, bulging travelling-rucksack with a clattering tin cup tied to it,

*rockets in the door and slides across the floor,
knocking over a lamp. Neil and Iona stare. Then enter
Kirsty, as if shot out of a cannon and landing on her
feet. She lands mid-stage.*

Kirsty Hello. It's me.

Iona (*looking at Neil*) Eh . . . Kirsty?

Kirsty Hi.

Neil Eh, come in, Kirsty.

Kirsty (*kicking the door shut with her foot, as Iona did
at the start*) I already am in.

Neil How are you?

*Neil has put his arm round Iona's shoulders. Iona puts
her arms round his waist. They're the perfect couple.
They beam at her, as if having their photograph taken.*

Kirsty I'm fine. How are you?

Iona Oh, we're really well.

Neil Really really good. Things are great here. Life just
gets better and better. How's yourself, Kirsty?

Kirsty I'm fine. (*laughingly*) How're you?

Neil We're fine.

Iona Yes . . . we're fine. How are – (*Stops herself.*)

Neil (*indicating the rucksack*) Off on your way somewhere
nice, Kirsty?

Kirsty No, I just got here, thanks.

*She sits down on the rucksack, gets out a mirror, looks
at herself, ruffles her hair, puts the mirror back into
the rucksack.*

Neil Eh . . . sit down, Kirsty.

Iona Can I get you anything? Are you thirsty, Kirsty? Thirsty, Kirsty!

Iona and Kirsty both break into giggles, like this is an old joke. Neil looks alarmed.

Neil Coffee? I can make us all a fresh cafetière. Or there's wine. Wine? White or red, Kirsty? We've a really nice red opened, we had some of it last night, it's very nice indeed, or I can open a bottle of Chardonnay, it's an organic one, very –

Kirsty Have you got any really unusual kind of tea?

Neil Unusual tea? We've jasmine, Earl Grey, Assam. We've peppermint or camomile, a couple of other kinds. What've we got, Iona?

Kirsty (*to herself*) Iona.

Iona We've lemon and ginger, lemon honey and ginger, nettle, raspberry, orange zinger, apple, apple and mango, apple orange and mango, raspberry apple orange and mango, mango and echinacea, echinacea by itself, blackcurrant, blackcurrant and vanilla, hibiscus, rosehip and licorice, passion fruit, starfruit and paw-paw.

Kirsty Oh no. I was meaning something really unusual.

Neil Well, Iona love, have we any really unusual kind of tea?

Kirsty Surprise me.

Iona No, I don't think so. I think we've only got the normal kind of unusual tea.

Kirsty Oh well. No thanks, then.

Iona Can we not get you anything? Anything at all? Something to eat, maybe?

Kirsty What I really fancy right now is some barbecued chicken. Have you anything like that?

Neil No. Have we, love?

Iona Eh, no. I don't think we have.

Kirsty Oh well, no, I'm fine then, thanks. (*She gets a book out of her rucksack, opens it in the middle and starts to read it.*)

Iona I could get a chicken out of the freezer. I could make a sauce.

Kirsty That'd be lovely. Cheers. (*Goes back to her book.*)

Neil (*to Iona, hissed*) Don't you dare do that.

Iona (*hissed back*) Why?

Neil Because what's she doing here?

Iona *I* don't know.

Neil What's she want?

Iona How should *I* know?

Kirsty I can hear you both. I'm not deaf.

Iona Neil was just wondering, he was just saying, we were just wondering what your plans were.

Kirsty (*to herself*) Neil.

Neil Yes, Kirsty?

Kirsty Nothing. I was just saying your name.

Neil The thing is, Kirsty. We weren't actually expecting anyone tonight.

Kirsty Life's a bitch. Just when you weren't actually expecting it. Just when you thought you were going to have a nice quiet night in doing nothing. Just when you thought it was all absolutely crystal clear –

Iona What was?

Kirsty Who you were.

Iona (*confused*) Oh.

Neil (*trying to bring the subject back*) And? Your plans are?

Kirsty Oh. Sorry. Are you talking to me?

Neil What are you planning?

Kirsty I'm not planning anything. (*to Iona*) That's a bit paranoid. He's very aggressive. (*to Neil*) I'm just sitting here, for fuck sake. I'm just quietly reading my book. (*to Iona*) I was thinking, if you don't defrost that chicken soon I won't get to eat anything tonight.

Iona Oh. Yes. I'll just go and . . .

She exits, through the back. Neil watches her go, not believing it.

Neil (*heavily sarcastic*) Kirsty, what exactly can we do for you?

Kirsty Chicken's fine, thanks. (*Sudden thought.*) A salad might be nice with it, like.

Neil Would you not be more comfortable sitting on a chair? And I could put your rucksack over by the door –

Kirsty Don't you touch my rucksack.

Neil I was just going to move it over there so it'll be ready for you when you go.

Kirsty Go where?

Neil When you go.

Kirsty (*calls*) Iona?

Iona (*from through the back*) Uh huh?

Kirsty I'm staying for a while, is that okay?

Iona (*from through the back*) Oh yes. That'd be lovely.

Kirsty smiles charmingly at Neil.

Neil We're both very busy, you know. Your sister's got four and a half case studies to do, and I've four of my own to get on with.

Kirsty Don't let me hold you up. On you go. I'm not needing any entertaining.

Neil No, what I mean is, I was wondering. How long –?

Kirsty (*stands up, stretches.*) Which is my room?

Neil Ah well, see, that's the thing, Kirsty. I'm awful sorry. But we don't really have a sparè room.

Iona (*coming through*) There's the study.

Neil Yes, love, but we need the study. We use the study all the time.

Iona That's true. We were just talking about it before you arrived.

Neil You absolutely can't stay in the study. I need to use it for work tonight.

Kirsty Okay. No problem. I'll just sleep on the floor in here. Plenty room.

Neil Ah, but we need through here too. When one of us uses the study, the other one works through here.

Kirsty I'll not be any bother.

Iona She'll not be any bother, Neil.

Neil is alarmed at Iona's capitulation.

Kirsty I'll be quiet as a mouse. You'll not hear a squeak out of me.

She sits down in Neil's chair and takes a mouth organ out of her pocket.

Iona It's just for a wee while, Neil. She'll be quiet as a mouse.

Kirsty starts playing the mouth organ. Neil shoots a maddened look at Iona. He makes a drama out of collecting his briefcase up and leaving the room by the back exit.
Iona is clearly terribly excited to have Kirsty here.

Iona I can't believe you're here. It's so lovely to see you.

Kirsty Uh huh, good, that's nice.

Iona It's been so long!

Kirsty It has, hasn't it?

Iona (*confidential*) I can't believe you swore at him.

Kirsty Did I?

Iona It feels so different tonight. Anything could happen.

Kirsty Super.

Iona I don't know what to say. We should talk. That's what sisters do, isn't it?

Kirsty Eh, oh yes, I suppose. I could do with just having a sleep, though, eh, what's your name again?

Iona Iona.

Kirsty Iona what?

Iona What do you mean, Iona what?

Kirsty Iona car? Iona house? Iona comfy-little-timeshare-somewhere-in-Tuscany? Iona stable-of-racehorses?

Iona Kirsty. You haven't changed a bit.

Kirsty Are you sure? Anyway, uh, Iona, I could really do with having a sleep. Seriously. I've been on the go for weeks.

Iona Oh right. Have you been away?

Kirsty Oh yes, all over the place.

Iona All over the place? I can't imagine. Where about?

Kirsty Everywhere. You name it.

Iona India? Africa? Nepal?

Kirsty Em, no.

Iona (*keen*) What kinds of things did you see on your travels?

Kirsty Oh, loads of things.

Iona What like?

Kirsty Well, last night I saw an elephant, right up close. I was so close to it that when it swished its tail, its tail hit me.

Iona Did it?

Kirsty And I saw a . . . man riding a bicycle that only had one wheel, and I saw a . . . girl walking on nothing but a rope, a really thin rope, miles up in the air, and . . . I saw the ponies that went round and round in a circle with people standing on their backs, and –

Iona I'd love to go travelling and see things. I'd love it. I wish that was the kind of life I had.

Kirsty (*yawning*) Oh, yes, it's great.

Iona But we can't, because of the mortgage. What do you think of the flat?

Kirsty Uh huh, it's nice, eh?

Iona (*desperate to please, looking for something to show Kirsty, showing her the salt-and-pepper grinder*) What do you think of this? We just got it today.

Kirsty Uh huh. It's very nice.

Kirsty grates some pepper out onto the floor. Iona is worried Neil will see, and runs to fetch a dustpan and brush. She sweeps it up.

Kirsty It works quite well, eh?

Iona We got it online. We buy a lot of things online.

Kirsty Why?

Iona I don't know. It's just easier.

Kirsty Easier?

Iona Easier than going to the shops. It's exciting. You pay for it on your credit card. So it doesn't seem like you're spending money at all. Then the next day or a few days later the thing you've bought comes through the door, like a present.

Kirsty A present from who?

Iona I don't know. I've never thought about it. A present from anyone. It just comes through the door. A present from God.

Kirsty A present from God – and you chose this? (*She holds up the salt-and-pepper grinder.*)

Iona (*sitting by Kirsty, settling down on the floor*) Do you remember when we were wee and after our bath on a Saturday night our mother would put us to bed, then you'd lie there next to me all night telling me all the stories, story after story, and we would try our hardest to stay awake as long as we could, and look at the stars and the moon and the morning coming up?

Kirsty Eh. No.

Iona No?

Kirsty To be honest. No.

Iona What do you mean, no?

Kirsty I don't remember any of that.

Iona (*shocked*) You don't? You don't remember lying there beside me telling me the stories? Story after story?

She looks at Kirsty for the first time as if she hardly knows her, as if Kirsty might be a stranger, as if she might call Neil through. Seeing this, Kirsty works fast.

Kirsty No. But. (*Storytelling.*) Listen. Did you know that this house, this flat, this very building, is built on the very place that the mysterious, legendary Highland seer, eh, Finn Finlay MacFinn, was born?

Iona A seer?

Kirsty Finlay Finn MacFinn, the man who could see into the future.

Iona (*transfixed*) Born here! Where we live!

Kirsty Yep.

Iona Tell me about him.

Kirsty Um. Most of what anyone knows about Finn MacFinn the great MacFinn comes from the eh, the oral tradition, stories that have been handed down and handed down, from mouth to ear, speaker to listener, for centuries.

Iona The oral tradition says that he was born here?

Kirsty Yep. On the very site of this building, according to ancient oral tradition, stood his mother's ancient cattle cot. Legend has it that he, he – (*She looks at the salt-and-pepper grinder in her hand.*) – that when he was a boy, one fateful day he gazed into his mother's salt-lick that she had for the cows –

Iona What's a salt-lick?

Kirsty It's a huge lump of salt, you know, for horses and cows to lick. Cows need salt. Otherwise, how would salt get into milk and butter?

Iona Oh. Right. What do horses need it for?

Kirsty Everything needs salt. We need it to live. Do you not want to know about the seer?

Iona Oh yes! I do! Tell me.

Kirsty And he gazed into the mists of the salt-lick, and he saw the future. 'This country will be at war with itself,' he said, 'and then it will be at peace.'

Iona He said that?

Kirsty Yep. And uh, 'This country will be bought with English gold by a parcel of rogues, but in the end it'll all be sorted out and all right again.'

Iona Amazing.

Kirsty From that day on, he carried the salt-lick everywhere with him and made many prophecies by looking into the mists of it. At first the salt-lick was quite heavy, being a big lump of salt, but then it rained, and snowed, and on the hot days his hands were sweaty, and of course animals were always, you know, running after him to get a lick of it, and as the years passed it got smaller and smaller, until Finn of the Salty Hands, as he was known locally, had almost no salt-lick left to look through.

Iona It dissolved!

Kirsty Yep. But legend has it that some of the salt from that salt-lick still exists in this part of the country, that it's there for people to find if they want, and, as Finn MacFinlay MacFinn himself said, 'The day will come when folk should watch very carefully what it is that they're putting in their soup.'

Iona Oh! That's so true! What other things did he foretell?

Kirsty Well. See, that's the thing. Some of them have come true and others haven't. Yet.

Iona Like what?

Kirsty For instance. He is reputed to have said: 'The day will come, and come it will, when it will be possible to make many purchases without visiting a shop. And when that faraway day comes, it will be possible to spend money that no human hand has ever touched.'

Iona I wonder what it means?

Kirsty plays nonchalantly with the salt-and-pepper grinder until she gets it.

Oh! It's – true!

Kirsty I can't believe we're supposed to be sisters. You're so slow.

Iona How d'you mean, you can't believe we're *supposed* to be s—

Kirsty (*quick*) And he is also reputed to have said – and this is one of his most famous reputed sayings – (*She speaks as if in a trance.*) 'In the days, the terrible days, when a country made anew cannot honour its differences, cannot hear the many, many different voices all singing together to make its one unique voice; in the days, the terrible days, when strangers will no longer be welcomed at the hearth of a Scottish home; the days, the terrible days, when sister will turn against sister and throw her out of her flat when she only wants somewhere to stay for a little while; ah, blessed I am not to see those days, for nothing shall follow them but calamity, calamity and selfishness all.'

Iona Amazing.

Kirsty I know. So true. The bit about the sister. It would be a terrible thing, wouldn't it?

Iona No, I mean the bit about hearing things.

Kirsty (*who can't really remember what she's said*) Oh yes, that bit, aye, that bit, exactly, that's amazing, eh?

Iona Because, you know, Kirsty – (*She looks behind her, making sure Neil isn't listening and can't hear her.*) I've been hearing things.

Kirsty What kind of things? Voices?

Iona Music. Scottish music. Every time I come home from work. Every time I open that door and come in. Every night. There it is, this music playing, playing really loud.

Kirsty Uh huh?

Iona And the thing is, it's not coming from anywhere. See, the Hendersons across the hall are away on holiday. Actually, we've never met the Hendersons, they keep themselves to themselves, like we do, but I'm sure there's nobody in their flat just now anyway.

Kirsty You've never met your neighbours?

Iona Actually, we've not met anybody else from this building. But that's quite normal now, in modern city living, isn't it?

Kirsty Is it?

Iona And the flat below us is empty, it's always been empty since we moved here. There's no flat above us, this is the top flat. And anyway, the music I hear is definitely not playing in the stairwell, or coming from below, or above, or the Hendersons' flat. It's only in here. And sometimes – sometimes later in the evening, and sometimes even in the morning – I think I can hear crowds of people.

Kirsty People?

Iona Laughing. Neil thinks I'm going mad. He says, next thing I'll be seeing things. But I'm telling you. I swear, music. I get home, and it's the music again. Every night I hear it playing. I don't know what to do about it.

Kirsty Have you tried dancing to it?

Iona Dancing . . . ?

Kirsty You know. Moving your arms and legs about in time to it?

Iona No.

Kirsty Or singing?

Iona Eh . . . no.

Kirsty Maybe it's wanting you to sing along with it.

Iona I never thought to try either of those things.

Kirsty Well, what *do* you do?

Iona I usually put on my own music, and that makes it stop.

Kirsty Then what happens?

Iona Well. Then I go through the back, then Neil comes home and picks up the stuff off the floor, then we have an argument about music, then I try to tell him about the Scottish music but he doesn't believe me, then we have another argument, about his golf clubs and the floor surface, then another one, about the toast this time, then we talk about work, then we argue about you, then we talk about how happy we are that nothing happens in our lives, then we sit quietly till it gets dark, till it gets light again and morning comes, and we have breakfast and start all over again.

Kirsty That's what you did tonight?

Iona That's what we do every night.

Kirsty Let me get this right. Every night –

Iona Everything starts when I come in and hear this music playing from nowhere.

Kirsty What kind of tune does it have?

Iona It's all different tunes. There's one that kind of goes . . . you know that one that goes – (*She hums a bit of 'The Lewis Bridal Song'.*)

Kirsty Oh, I know, I know. Is it –? (*She starts playing it on her mouth organ.*)

Iona Yes! That's it!

Iona jumps up, clapping. Kirsty plays. Until Neil comes striding through, face like thunder, and snatches it away from her mouth. He puts it in his pocket, with distaste.

Kirsty Give me that back!

Iona Neil! Neil! Listen to this! Our flat is built right on top of where the cottage where Finn the great MacFinn, the seer who could look into the future through his mother's salt-lick, was born!

Neil Who?

Iona He saw everything! He saw the, what was it, the packet of rogues, and he saw that it would just come through the door with no money!

Neil What?

Kirsty gets another mouth organ out of her pocket. She's about to put it to her mouth when Neil sees and snatches it away like before.

Neil No!

Kirsty You can't put a stop to me just 'cause you don't like the noise I make, you know.

Iona And he saw – eh, what else did he see, Kirsty? He saw voices, all coming together!

Kirsty gets another mouth organ out of her pocket and holds it up for him to take.

Kirsty (*to Neil*) I don't know about you but I can go on doing this all night.

Neil Iona. Ask your sister to stop making a noise while I'm trying to work.

Kirsty What kind of work is it you actually do, Neil?

Neil It's none of your business.

Kirsty (*to Iona instead*) What kind of work is it he actually does, Iona?

Iona Neil and I both do the same kind of work, Kirsty, you know that.

Neil Iona. Don't tell her anything. (*to Kirsty*) It's confidential.

Kirsty (*to Iona*) But you can tell *me*.

Neil Iona . . .

Iona There's no harm. She's my sister. (*to Kirsty*) We do those case studies. You know.

Kirsty What kind of case studies?

Iona (*realising for the first time that she doesn't really know*) Well. Studies.

Kirsty Of . . .?

Iona . . . cases?

Kirsty You don't know, do you? You don't know what it is you're supposed to be doing. Neither of you knows.

Neil Iona, I can smell burning.

Iona I can't.

Neil The chicken.

Iona Oh. The chicken.

Exit Iona by the back.

Neil Right.

Kirsty Just you and me, eh, Neil? Just you and me. Come on, then. Outside. Now. If you think you're hard enough.

Neil (*shocked*) I'm not fighting a girl!

Kirsty Scared you might lose? Eh? Eh?

Neil No decent man would ever hit a girl.

Kirsty Scared your wife'll see you knocked out cold, floored by a girl?

Neil (*as if his ears have pricked up*) Ye – es. Yes. That's right. I don't want my *wife* to be hurt by me hitting her *sister*.

Kirsty You're just jealous I'm not *your* sister.

Neil Yes, that you're my *wife*'s sister.

Kirsty You're just jealous there's no sister here to stick up for *you*.

35

Neil (*dissembling, making Kirsty uneasy*) Yes. I'm just disappointed that we're not all better friends. After we all had such a good time together at the wedding.

Kirsty Oh yeah. Yes, we did, didn't we?

Neil Remember the wedding? By wedding, just to make it clear, I mean the wedding where your sister Iona and I got married, you remember?

Kirsty Yes. I'm not stupid.

Neil What are your special memories of that special day, Kirsty?

Kirsty Oh, I remember everything. How could I forget? What an unforgettable day.

Neil Remember how we laughed when your bridesmaid's dress caught on the door and someone had to go and get your mother to come and cut you free with a pair of pinking shears?

Kirsty Oh yes. How we laughed.

Neil And do you remember how we danced?

Kirsty All night, some of us. What a night it was.

Neil And Kirsty, do you remember your own shocked face, when I sneaked up behind you, and –

Kirsty And –?

Neil – whispered in your ear –

Kirsty Uh huh, go on –

Neil is now standing intimately right behind Kirsty, right up against her.

Neil (*stage whisper*) – that special thing that I wanted only you to know about?

Kirsty (*nodding, lost, stage-whispering too*) Uh huh, oh yes, the secret.

Neil (*stage whisper*) That Iona and I aren't married?

Kirsty (*stage whisper*) What a modern couple you are.

Neil (*stage whisper*) That there never was a wedding day? That you're a little liar, and a little usurper, and that you've been found out?

Kirsty (*stage whisper*) Usurper's an awful big word for it.

Neil (*still standing very close to Kirsty, his head right by her ear, roars deafeningly*) Iona?

Iona (*appearing in the back doorway with an apron on*) Yes?

Neil This person isn't your sister.

Iona Not my sister?

Kirsty Don't listen to him. He's going to try to turn you against me.

Neil She's a vagabond. A vicious vagrant. A . . . a . . .

Kirsty Something else beginning with 'v'?

Neil I don't know what she is.

Kirsty Vignette? Vegan? Velocipede?

Neil Don't listen to her. I think she might be mad.

Kirsty *You* think *I* might be mad?

Neil A thief too, maybe. We should check her pockets. See if anything's missing from the flat. I knew from the start there was something funny about her. We should never have let her in the door.

Iona Neil! Don't talk about family like that.

Neil She's not. I don't know what or who she is, I don't know where she's come from, but I do know this. She's nothing to do with us.

Kirsty He's going to tell you I'm a – what was it, Neil? Usurper.

Neil She *is* a usurper.

Iona (*to Kirsty*) Your supper's fine. The chicken wasn't burnt at all.

Neil Not your supper. Usurper.

Iona I know. I'm not stupid.

Kirsty He'll be telling you I'm a liar next.

Neil She is! She's a liar! She thought we were married!

Iona Well, it's an easy mistake to make, we are very close, Neil.

Kirsty That's what *I* said.

Neil No, no, because when *I* told her there'd been a wedding day and dancing and God knows what else –

Iona But Neil. We agreed not to get married till we were both a bit more settled. (*to Kirsty*) There hasn't been a wedding day.

Kirsty I know. He's such a liar.

Neil No, it's her that's the liar, listen, listen, because when I told her a made up story, a thing I just made up on the spur of the moment, that her bridesmaid's dress had caught on a door, she kidded on she knew what I was talking about!

Kirsty I was just being polite. I hadn't a clue what he was on about.

Iona See? It's an easy mistake to make. She was just being polite.

Kirsty (*to Neil*) Fucking weirdo.

Neil Don't you ever curse at me again, d'you hear?

Kirsty Don't you ever try to come between me and my sister again, d'you hear?

Neil She's not your sister.

Iona *Neil.* No, but you shouldn't swear, Kirsty. Cursy Kirsty.

They both laugh giggly laughs. Neil looks ready to explode.

Iona (*putting her arm round Kirsty*) Not my sister. Imagine. When we're so alike.

Neil goes to sit in his armchair, in the huff.

Kirsty (*to Iona*) Would you like me to teach you some swears?

Iona (*confidential*) Neil hates me doing it.

Neil has opened the newspaper he brought in with him, and is reading it, sullenly.

Kirsty Course he does. Because swearing is actually a form of magic.

Iona (*enthralled*) How do you mean?

Kirsty Exactly. How do you mean.

Iona How d'you mean, how do you mean?

Kirsty Swears are very powerful. That's why people are still shocked to hear other people use them. They're words that are loaded with power. Some people don't like certain other people having too much power in their words, or in the way they live, or in the way they are.

Iona (*lost*) Uh huh?

Kirsty (*knowing the way to persuade Iona*) Take the seer I was telling you about earlier, Finn MacFinlay Finlayson. He knew the power of the things that people don't want to hear.

Iona Oh yes. Yes, I see.

Kirsty He told the society of his day things that they didn't want to have to know, about the future, and about themselves.

Iona Things like what?

Kirsty So do you want me to teach you some swears now? Because I know some really good ones.

Iona I'd rather you told me more about the seer. For instance, what happened when he told his society the things they didn't want to hear, the things that couldn't be said out loud? Did they thank him? Were they relieved? Were they delighted that things and society and people could be seen more clearly now because of what he'd told them?

Neil, who has been rattling his newspaper through the last conversation, turns a page and suddenly lets out a yelp of delight, jumping in his seat.

Kirsty (*unsettled by Neil*) Well, the thing about society and seers is that, is that –

Iona What?

Neil stands up. Strides to the middle of the stage. Kirsty is watching him, wary.

Kirsty They generally don't get along.

Neil (*folding his newspaper, to read out of it, clears his throat*) 'Police are anxious to trace the whereabouts of Janie MacDougall, pictured above, known under various aliases including Mirabella of the Marvels, Fortuna the Fabulous High-Wire-Walker and Sybilla-I-See-Everything. Most recently known to be working as recently as last month at Herring Bros Circus, under the name Maestra the Magnificent Mindreading Act, Ms MacDougall (twenty-seven) is wanted urgently by police to answer accusations of mountebankery, absconding with five nights of Herring Bros takings, and questions on a series of cases of attempted frauds all over the country, whose total cash haul is estimated to be in the region of two hundred and forty thousand pounds.'

At the last bit, Kirsty guffaws. Neil turns the paper round so Iona can see the picture. Iona takes the paper from him.

Iona Oh! Kirsty! It's a picture of you!

Neil See?

Kirsty You shouldn't believe everything you read in the papers.

Neil I told you. What did I tell you?

Iona But it says here your name is – that you have lots of names.

Kirsty That's the thing about me. I've got a very fluid sense of self.

Neil What did I tell you? What did I say?

Iona So – are you not Kirsty, then?

Kirsty Well, I am. And, to be honest, I'm not.

Iona And what about all this money?

Kirsty Oh please. Do I look like a person with two hundred and forty thousand pounds to my name – er, names?

Iona I can't believe you'd lie to me. I can't believe my own sister would – (*Stops, sudden realisation.*) I can't believe my own sister.

Neil It's a hundred times better, a hundred times worse than I thought. I had her pegged as a vagrant. I thought somewhere in my far-too-open heart that I was being unfair asking someone to leave my house who might have nowhere to go for the night. But now. Now. You come in here pretending to be family. You worm your way in, cheat your way into my house.

Iona Our house, Neil.

Neil Our house. You sham and cheat and lie and fake your way into our hospitality.

Kirsty (*shrugging*) So?

Neil So? So? So I think it's finally time you left.

Kirsty (*mainly for Iona's benefit, though with a finger pointing at Neil*) Before you throw me from your hearth, take a moment to remember the tragic end of Finlay MacFinn MacFinlayson, the seer born right here in your very house, maybe born on this very, very spot I'm standing on.

Neil In mid air?

Iona What tragic end?

Neil Iona, don't be fooled. It's a trick.

Iona But what happened?

Kirsty What happened was this – the great seer MacFinn met his tragic end when he was thrown from the land and the bosom of his cheap and disbelieving people. 'You are no longer family,' they told him. 'You are a sham, a cheat, a liar and a fake.'

Iona Oh!

Kirsty Their very words. And the great seer Finn rose to his full height then, of six and a half feet, and raised his salt-lick to his eye for the last time, and for the last time spoke his final last words in the world: 'You will be cursed with loneliness when I go, and cursed with sameness and monotony. You will be cursed with living unseasoned lives. And anybody in the centuries yet to come after my demise in a minute, who rejects someone like me, as you have done to me, will be cursed exactly the same –'

Iona Cursed?

Neil Oh for goodness sake.

Kirsty '– cursed they'll be, with the hearing of a music they no longer understand. The laughter of ghosts will be in their uncomprehending ears.'

Silence.

Iona Then what happened to him?

Kirsty Then they hung, drew and quartered him and tortured him and flayed him and impaled him and burned him alive. And that, eventually, was the end of the legendary great seer, Finn MacFinn of the MacFinns.

Iona Oh!

Kirsty Nobody likes to receive the message of a seer.

Neil Finished your speech?

He gets Kirsty by the shoulders, ready to eject her.

Iona Neil. Neil. Don't. We can't throw her out. We don't want to be cursed.

Neil Iona, don't be ridiculous.

Iona But listen. Just listen for a minute. I remembered something else that that seer said. Calamity will follow when a sister turns against a sister and throws her out of a flat.

Neil The seer is made up. It's a load of rubbish. And anyway. She's not your sister.

Iona I'm not wanting any calamity, Neil, regardless of whether she's my sister or not. And that seer was born here, she said.

Kirsty (*to Iona*) Don't worry. It's just a story. Nothing bad'll happen to you. (*to Neil*) It's okay. I'm going, I'm going. I know when I'm not wanted.

Neil has picked up her rucksack.

Neil It's rustly, like it's full of paper. I think it's full of banknotes.

Kirsty Don't touch that.

He holds it out insolently, drops it at her feet. For the first time in the play, Kirsty gets angry.

Careful with that, for fuck sake. That's everything I own in the world in there.

The tin cup on the side of the rucksack clatters off it, off the front of the stage.

My cup. Oh no. My cup. Where's my cup g— ?

Neil (*standing over by the door, holding it open*) Out. Now. Show's over.

But Kirsty, who has followed the path of the cup, is staring with her mouth open straight out, at the audience. For the first time she can see them. She is astounded. She stands as if in a trance.

Come on!

44

Iona What's the matter with her?

Kirsty Who – who are *they*?

Iona Why is she staring at the wallpaper like that?

Neil We were seconds away from getting our house back to ourselves . . .

Kirsty All those people.

Iona What people?

Kirsty Who are they?

Neil It's a trick. How many times do I have to tell you? It's just a trick.

Kirsty (*turns to Neil and Iona, face shining*) Look!

Iona (*going over to look*) Look at what?

Neil Oh, for God's sake.

Iona (*peering*) I can't see anybody. It's just the wall, Kirsty. (*Back over her shoulder, to Neil.*) D'you think I should still be calling her Kirsty? (*to Kirsty*) There's nobody there. There's nothing.

Kirsty All the people! Sitting in the dark!

Iona I think she's seeing faces in the wallpaper.

Kirsty Rows and rows of them. Sitting in – chairs. Who do you think they are?

Neil (*shutting the front door, leaning on it*) I don't believe this.

Kirsty What do you think they want?

Iona She's shivering. She's shaking all over. Is it faces in the wallpaper, Kirsty?

Neil Don't encourage her.

Iona What kind of faces? Happy faces?

Kirsty I can't make out any faces. At least, not yet . . . dark out there.

Iona (*feels Kirsty's head, takes her pulse*) She's burning up. She's got a real temperature. Her pulse is going mad.

Neil marches over, gets Iona by the arm. He looks at Kirsty, and is unnerved by her. She is shining and strange. He drags Iona over to the other side of the room, pushes her down into her armchair.

Neil If you'd let me handle this, she'd be gone by now. But no. We had to do it your way.

Iona Look. She's clearly not well, Neil.

Neil It's an act, for crying out loud. An act. She's putting on an act. Haven't you understood anything about what's happening to us tonight?

Kirsty (*still staring out*) Wow!

She sinks down cross-legged on the floor, still trying to make out the audience.

Iona (*shaking her head*) I'm worried, Neil. She's ill. She needs looking after.

Neil (*a little more convinced that this might be too big for him to handle*) She needs putting away.

Iona I'll make her a cup of tea and a hot water bottle. Then we'll decide what to do for the best. And I'll keep calling her Kirsty just now. It might upset her to be called something else. Uh – Kirsty, would you like a nice cup of tea?

Kirsty (*still engrossed*) Eh . . . no thanks.

Neil I think we should phone the police.

Iona Or maybe an ambulance. Maybe the mental hospital. After all, she's not actually my sister, is she?

Neil (*pleased – they're a team again*) No.

Iona Even if she was. We've got to do the right thing.

Neil Exactly. I'll phone the police.

Iona Wait.

Neil They're looking for her anyway. It said.

Iona No. A doctor. Look at her. The shock of being found out is maybe what's upset her. A cup of tea, calm her down. I'll make one. You keep an eye on her. And don't bully her, Neil. People in her state are very fragile. She could do anything.

Neil I won't. I promise.

> *Exit Iona at the back. But Neil can't resist it. He goes to his jacket. He takes his phone out of the pocket. He goes over to Kirsty. Her strangeness is still unnerving him, but he makes himself brave and squats down beside her on his haunches.*

You have thirty seconds to vacate my flat, Marvella the Mysterious. In thirty seconds I'm calling the police.

> *Without looking round even, and with the slightest of movements, Kirsty manages to take the phone from Neil and push him so he loses his balance and falls over backwards. While he's on his back and fussing about getting up, she's opened the phone, taken out its battery, flicked the battery over the edge of the stage, watching it fall, delighted, and closed the phone again. When he's back on his feet, she's ready for him, holding out the phone, still with her eyes on the audience.*

Neil (*a bit scared*) What did you do to my phone?

47

Kirsty I'm definitely not going anywhere now. It's got so interesting here.

Neil examines his phone, trying to get it to work. Suddenly –

You!

Neil (*jumps*) What?

But Kirsty is standing now, and is pointing out at the audience.

Kirsty You. Say something.

Neil (*worried, calling*) Iona . . . ?

Kirsty Talk to me. I won't bite.

Iona (*coming through, cup of tea in her hand*) What's happening?

Neil She broke the phone.

Iona Let me see it.

Neil I can't phone the police, the hospital, anyone.

Kirsty *You*, then?

Neil She keeps shouting. Like that. She's gone mad. I think she's gone mad.

Iona (*shaking the phone*) How will we get help for her now?

Neil How will we get help for ourselves?

Kirsty (*still glued to audience*) You could always ask the Hendersons across the hall.

Neil Yes! The Hendersons! Oh no, that's right – the Hendersons are away.

Kirsty Oh no, that's right – the Hendersons don't exist.

Iona What does she mean, the Hendersons don't exist?

Kirsty Have you ever seen the Hendersons? No? Well, then.

Iona It is odd, Neil, isn't it, that we've never actually seen the Hendersons?

Neil Not at all. The Hendersons are probably a busy working couple, exactly like us. They probably go off to work in the morning, come home in the evening, then get up the next morning to go to work. Our paths never cross, that's all. And they're away a lot, they probably work abroad.

Kirsty Are the Hendersons a figment of your collective imagination? Basic philosophy, lesson number one – ready? If the Hendersons are sitting by themselves in a dark room, with nobody thinking about them, are they still the Hendersons? And – the big question – if you've never seen the Hendersons, have the Hendersons never seen you?

Iona I don't know. Have they, Neil?

Neil How would I know? I don't know.

Kirsty And if they haven't ever seen you, how do you know not just that the Hendersons themselves exist, but that *you* do?

Neil But –

Iona Oh my God. Neil, do we exist?

Neil Of course we exist!

Iona But how do we know?

Neil Look. You can hear me, you can see me, can't you? She can hear us and see us.

Iona Yes. But –

Neil She's trying to make us as mad as her.

Iona What'll we do? What'll we do if we don't exist?

Neil The best thing to do with a mad person, in a phoneless situation like ours, is to . . . ignore them. Until they go away of their own accord.

Iona Right. Right. Ignore her. How?

Neil Well, we just go on with our evening, as if there's nobody else here.

Iona But there is.

Neil Yes, I *know*. But we *act* like there *isn't*.

Iona What – like, pretend we're by ourselves?

Kirsty (*to audience*) How am I going to get you to talk to me?

Iona Pretend we didn't hear that?

Neil Worth a try.

Iona Okay. Let's try.

They both sit in their armchairs, as if by themselves.

Iona Right. You first.

Neil (*sighs and yawns*) Soon be time for bed.

Iona Yes, then time to get up and have breakfast and go to work again.

Iona suddenly realises she's got a cup of tea in her hand, which she'd made for Kirsty.

Oh. But what about this . . . this cup of tea I made for *you*, Neil.

Neil Thank you, love.

Iona Pleasure, love.

Neil (*sips it, makes a face*) Ugh. No sugar. How could you make me a cup of tea and not put sugar in it?

Iona (*irate*) I didn't make it for you, I made it for – (*Stops herself.*) I'll just nip through and put some sugar in it for you. Sorry, I forgot.

Neil Thank you, love.

Exit Iona by the back. Neil stalwartly pretends that Kirsty isn't there.

Kirsty I know! I know! I know what to do.

She takes a blindfold out of her rucksack. Just before she puts it on herself, she turns to Neil.

Kirsty (*to Neil*) If you touch me while I'm wearing this. If you come anywhere near me. I'll stamp on your phone till it's all in little bits. And I'll never leave.

Neil completely ignores her. But as the following happens, he starts watching, surreptitiously.
With the blindfold on, Kirsty stands mid-stage, facing the audience.

Kirsty Ladies and gentlemen. Count yourselves lucky. Count yourselves blessed.

I, Maestra the Magnificent, am here among you tonight to prove once and for all that the uncanny can happen. And to reveal to you the mysterious marvellous multifariousness of the totally unseen invisible veiled connections that run between all of us all the time. For as you sit there before me, though you don't know it, secret messages are transmitting themselves from you to me. Yes they are. I can prove it. Tonight I will amaze and amuse you, shock, surprise and stimulate you, and all simply by telling you several very personal facts – things, ladies and gentlemen, that you will agree, there is no way on earth that I could have known about you.

Are you ready to have yourselves revealed to you out of the darkness? For the performance of this extraordinary feat, all I ask of you is your patience, your truthfulness and your complete silence, while I concentrate as hard as I must to bring your minds and selves to mine.

Holds her forehead. Trance.

Ladies and gentlemen. There is someone among you tonight who is wearing a watch on the wrist of his or her left arm. You know who you are, stand up – (*to herself, shaking her head*) Too many.

Holds her forehead. Trance.

Ladies and gentlemen. There is someone among you tonight – you will know who you are – who comes from a house where the front room curtains are needing a bit of a wash. Stand up! Stand up! (*to herself*) Still too many. Narrow in a bit.

Holds her forehead. Trance.

Ladies and gentlemen. There is someone among you tonight – you will know who you are – who earlier this evening had kippers fried in garlic for their tea. (*to herself*) Yuch.

Holds her forehead. Trance.

Ladies and gentlemen, eh, no offence to the lady who ate the kippers, don't stand up, I'm going to choose someone else . . . ah, ah, wait. Yes. Ladies and gentlemen, there is someone among you tonight – you will know who you are – who is sitting beside an empty seat. It is an empty seat which was kept for a friend who was supposed to come tonight but didn't turn up . . . and the name of that friend who didn't turn up . . . is . . . Janice. (*to herself*) Yes. That's it. (*to them*) Stand up, friend of Janice. I'm talking to you, and you alone. You have been chosen.

She takes off the blindfold, comes out of her mind-reading state.

Have I done it? have I made contact with anyone?

Voice from Audience Yes. Me.

Kirsty (*excited, and panicked*) Oh my God. It worked. It worked. It's never worked before. It worked.

She dances round the stage. Dances round Neil's chair. Neil ignores her steadfastly.

It worked! It worked! (*to person in audience*) I can hear you! I can hear you as well as see you!

Voice from Audience (*it's an English voice*) Do you want me just to keep standing?

Kirsty Yes! No – actually, what I want is for you to come down here and bring me my cup back.

Voice from Audience What? Um . . .

Kirsty Come where I can see you. Come into the light, come into the light. Do not be afraid. And bring my cup. It's there. It fell.

Voice from Audience What – you want me to come there?

Kirsty Yes. Come on. Come on. You can do it.

Voice from Audience Oh no. No, I can't do that. You could just nip down off the stage yourself and get it.

Kirsty I can't come out there!

Voice from Audience Why?

Kirsty I'd maybe die. And I really really really need my cup back. It's almost all I've got in the world. Please. Please come. Please bring my cup. It's an heirloom. It was handed down to me from my mother's mother's mother's mother. It's precious to me. I chose you. You're the messenger. The fates chose you to bring me back my cup.

Voice from Audience (*Sabrina*) All right. Hang on.

Kirsty Hurray hurray hurray!

Sabrina goes, laughing, nervous, self-conscious, to pick up the cup. She gets up on stage and stands as people do when they've been persuaded up by pantomime characters to sing a song, or by hypnotists – gawky, embarrassed, beaming, squinting in the lights. She is wearing good quality hippy-looking clothes. When Sabrina enters stage, Neil spasms. He is terrified.

Neil Oh bloody hell! Oh for fuck –! Oh shit oh shit oh shit –

He hides behind his chair, peeking over the top. Sabrina and Kirsty regard him.

Kirsty Strong words. (*to Sabrina*) You did that.

Sabrina He's so uptight. I kept thinking while I was watching, he could really do with a detox massage.

Kirsty Never mind him just now. Thanks for this. (*Takes cup, throws it over her shoulder.*)

Sabrina If I'd known you were going to do that with it I wouldn't have bothered to come all the way up onto the stage with it.

Kirsty Onto the what with it?

Sabrina gestures, arms out.

Never mind. Let's talk about you. What's your name?

Sabrina Sabrina.

Kirsty What an unusual name.

Sabrina I know. It's embarrassing. It's from *Charlie's Angels*.

Kirsty So you're an angel.

Sabrina The year I was born *Charlie's Angels* was my mother's favourite TV programme and one of the characters in it was called Sabrina and she liked the name so she called me it.

Kirsty And is Charlie the god you belong to?

Sabrina It's a TV programme. You must know it.

Kirsty I'm Kirsty, well, Maestra the Magnificent, and that's Neil.

Sabrina I know. I was out there, watching.

Kirsty You were watching? It's true, then, that we are not alone?

Sabrina How did you know about Janice? That's amazing, really. I'm really impressed.

Kirsty And that's where you live – 'out there'?

Sabrina Well, in a manner of speaking. Locally.

Kirsty In the other world.

Sabrina Em –

Kirsty What's it like where you're from?

Sabrina Well, I live in ——— (*name of village near theatre*).

Kirsty What's ———?

Sabrina It's a village a few miles from here, I've got a cottage there, I've just bought it. Property's still reasonably inexpensive up there.

Kirsty And you live 'up there'?

Sabrina I'm not originally from there, I'm an incomer. I moved up there three years ago.

Kirsty An incomer?

Sabrina Yes. I run a small non-profit-making business. I make and sell dream-catchers.

Kirsty You make and sell what?

Sabrina Dream-catchers. You know. They're made out of wood and thread, coloured thread, like a web or a net.

Kirsty Like for catching fish?

Sabrina Well, no. You put them under your pillow or hang them above your bed, and they catch your dreams. If you have bad dreams they weed them out before they get to you, catch them in their web.

Kirsty And people buy these? For money?

Sabrina They're not very expensive! Well, one I made was huge, that one was expensive, it was for a festival. I do a whole range, but they're usually about five pounds. The big one I made I actually got forty-five pounds for. It was the size of this stage.

Kirsty This what?

Sabrina I do some psychotherapeutic massage, that brings in a little money. And Alexander Technique.

Kirsty (*looking out at audience*) And where is Alexander Technique? Is he here tonight? Is he your boyfriend?

Sabrina No! It's a relaxation technique. Look, I'll show you. If you just push your spine in here, and your neck, do this – look.

Kirsty Oh! That's quite good.

Sabrina (*indicating Neil*) He's got terrible posture. Or it's maybe method acting, I don't know. Anyway, he needs help. (*to Neil*) If you walk like that all the time, when you're in your late forties you'll have really bad back trouble. You ought to do something about it soon. (*to Kirsty*) If I could just –

She goes towards Neil with her massage-hands out. Neil, who has been watching like a stricken rabbit, backs off and runs away, ducks behind the chair. At this point Iona enters, with a cup and saucer in her hand again.

Iona looks at Sabrina and Neil in amazement, not sure if she's supposed to be still ignoring Kirsty or not.

Iona I didn't hear the door.

Kirsty This is Iona.

Sabrina I know. Hello.

Kirsty She hears mysterious music coming from somewhere. (*to Iona*) This is Sabrina.

Iona What a night it's been for visitors here.

Kirsty Would you like a cup of tea, Sabrina?

Sabrina Is it organic?

Iona Um . . . yes.

Sabrina Was it an unbleached teabag?

Iona No, I don't think so.

Sabrina Oh well, no thanks.

Iona What a night it's been for people not wanting tea.

Kirsty Sabrina catches dreams. She's an angel who can make everything relax. She says Neil has terrible posture and that something will have to change.

Iona (*going over to Neil*) She talks funny.

Neil She's a ghost.

Iona She can't be a ghost. I just spoke to her and she spoke back. She sounds kind of English.

Neil I'm telling you. I saw her come through that wall. She put her arms and her legs and her head through it and she came into the room.

Sabrina It's nice up here. It's a really nice flat.

Iona Thank you. It's nice of you to say.

Sabrina I like the design. It's really fashionable. It feels really real.

Iona (*to Neil*) What do you think that means, really real?

Neil I don't know. Maybe it's a ghost term for really cool or something.

Iona (*to Sabrina*) Your jacket's 'really real' too.

Sabrina Oh, this old thing. I got it in an antique shop. I like your flooring.

Iona (*pleased*) Do you?

Sabrina It's really nice. But you shouldn't have your waste-paper basket by the door. In Feng Shui terms that means that nothing but rubbish will come in.

Iona Oh! (*Runs to move it.*)

Sabrina But it's nice up here. I've never been in a play before. Well, I've been in a play, but, you know, never been 'in' a play.

Kirsty In a what?

Sabrina I have to say though, this isn't at all the kind of play I thought it would be.

Iona The kind of . . . ?

Kirsty How do you mean?

Sabrina (*sitting down at the table, getting involved*) The characterisation of those two – (*She indicates Iona and Neil.*) – it's quite sexist and slight. Especially Neil. He's very slight.

Neil What's the ghost saying about me?

Kirsty She says you're slight.

Neil I'm slight? She's a ghost! She doesn't even exist!

Sabrina (*to Kirsty*) And *you're* not mentioned in the programme at all.

Kirsty In the what?

Sabrina The programme. (*She gets her programme out of her back pocket.*) Look.

> *She reads out the name of the play, the characters and their actors, the director, etc, with Neil and Iona interjecting – what can it mean that they're 'played' by someone?*

And the other thing, while I'm up here. I really disagree with you about what you call the 'power' of swearing. What you see as power I see as totemish adolescent overreaching.

Kirsty Eh?

Sabrina Swearing is nothing but a weak excuse for inarticulacy. It's degrading. It's a disappointment to those of us who wish for a better, cleaner, less troubled and vulgar world. Of course, there are always times when we need to let off steam, when we need to address things adolescently, on a profane pitch. But on the whole people just use swears and curses as a reason not to construct their syntax, and therefore themselves, properly. It's a semantic, and so a symbolic, avoidance of the responsibility we all have as human beings to each of our societies.

Kirsty I'm beginning to wish I'd spoken to someone else out there.

Sabrina And you're very guilty of it. You swear all the time, as a supposed marker of your anarchy. But it's not anarchic. It's not even clever.

Kirsty I'm even beginning to wish I'd spoken to the person who ate the fish.

Sabrina Actually all of you in this play are acting irresponsibly. There's a lot that needs sorting out up here.

While she's saying this, somewhere in the audience a mobile phone starts playing. Sabrina recognises its tune.

Sabrina Oh! I think that's mine. I'm so embarrassed, now everyone will know I've got a mobile.

Kirsty There are mobiles in the other world, too?

Iona I can hear a phone. Can you hear a phone?

Sabrina Could someone maybe answer it? It's there right on the top of my bag. You just press the button at the bottom –

An audience member answers it. A voice on the phone tells him or her to pass on the message to Sabrina that 'It's Janice, she's sorry she's late, and she'll try and get there for the beginning of the second act.'

Sabrina (*to audience member*) Thank you! She's always late. She doesn't really like theatre.

Kirsty Theatre?

Sabrina Not like I do. She always wants to talk through them. It's embarrassing. I don't really know why we're friends, we're quite different. She's quite a material person, as opposed to a spiritual one. Not that I'm being judgemental about what's better, material or spiritual. It's important to be both.

Neil Ask the ghost what kind of a phone it's got.

Sabrina See, that's exactly what I mean. That's really sexist characterisation.

Iona Neil's not sexist. Are you, Neil?

Neil No.

Iona Or slight. And we do exist. Don't we, Neil?

Neil (*feeble*) Yes.

Iona And the Hendersons. The Hendersons also exist. They're just away. On their holidays.

Sabrina That's a really commendable characteristic, sticking up for the underdog. I like that in your character.

Iona (*pleased*) Thanks.

Kirsty (*ignoring them*) What does that mean, she'll try and get here for the second act? What's the second act?

Sabrina Well. This is the first act. A play is usually in acts, sometimes three, sometimes five. This one has two acts. That's what it says in the programme.

Kirsty (*reading*) The play will be split into two acts, both lasting an hour, with an interval of fifteen minutes. An interval?

Sabrina Yes. (*Looks at her watch.*) According to my watch at least, this act should be ending any minute now.

Blackout.

Act Two

Lights up. Everybody is standing in exactly the same position as when the lights went down, but Iona, Neil and Kirsty look a little raddled, weary, their hair sticking up as if they've been up all night. They all blink – the lights are too bright. Then they carry on talking as if the interval's hardly been there.

Kirsty So if that was the first act, then according to you this must be –

Sabrina The second act. And not just according to me. According to the laws and traditions of theatre.

Kirsty Oh, I get it. Theatre is the name of the place out there, where you come from?

Sabrina No, no, you don't understand. *This* is theatre. This. Here. Now. You.

Kirsty Eh?

Neil (*to Iona, feeble*) Isn't this, here, now, usually the time we're having our breakfast?

Iona Would you like me to fetch some breakfast for you? It wouldn't take a minute. I could get breakfast for everybody.

Kirsty Huh. Fat chance. (*to Sabrina*) Don't expect to get anything to eat here. I never even got my barbecued chicken yet and I asked for that twelve hours ago.

Iona Oh, that'll be cold by now. It's been waiting for you on the sideboard for hours, since last night. I'll heat it up for you tonight.

Neil Is she still going to be here *tonight*?

Iona (*changing the subject*) Neil? What would you like?

Neil (*shaking his head, feeble*) I'm just not hungry this morning. I've no appetite at all. Everything is so . . . different today.

Sabrina A chicken has a face.

Kirsty Eh?

Sabrina You really shouldn't eat anything that has a face. Imagine. That chicken waiting for you on the sideboard once had a face. Eyes it looked out of. A nose. A mouth.

Kirsty You mean a beak.

Sabrina Sorry?

Kirsty It's not called a chicken nose and mouth, not here where we live, anyway. It's called a beak.

Sabrina I don't mean to be confrontational, but the words are relative. It's still a face.

Iona (*to Sabrina*) Would you like some breakfast? We have some food that doesn't have a face.

Sabrina Nothing for me, thanks. I'm fine, I just had my supper a couple of hours ago. It's still early evening for me.

Kirsty (*sitting cross-legged at Sabrina's feet, as if for a story*) Tell us some stories about the other world. What's it like on the other side? What's it like through the wall? Do you ever see God? What's God like?

Sabrina God? This is the twenty-first century. God is an outmoded patriarchal construct.

Kirsty Is He? Oh. Right.

Neil I feel . . . weak.

Iona (*concerned*) Do you?

Neil I feel a bit . . . sick.

Kirsty (*moving away*) Is he going to *be* sick?

Sabrina Put your head between your knees. Deep breaths. Sips of water.

Iona Would you like some water, love?

Neil I don't want anything. I don't know anything. A little while ago I was a man, I had a life, a good job, a flat, a relationship. Now I don't know anything. Everything is changed.

Sabrina Classic signs. He's having a personality fragmentation.

Iona A what?

Sabrina He needs to talk to an expert. I can give you the numbers of some good people to phone.

Neil (*groaning*) Oh! My phone!

Sabrina The statistics for this happening to men these days are rocketing sky high.

Iona (*putting her arms round him*) Kirsty, or whatever your name is, would you go through to the kitchen for me and bring him back a glass of water?

Kirsty No.

Iona I can't leave him.

Kirsty (*to Sabrina*) So . . . if your God is a – what was it? Outboard-motor – ?

Sabrina Outmoded patriarchal construct.

Kirsty Yes. If your God is that – then . . . then who made you?

Iona Please? Kirsty? Do it for me. Since we were, you know, family once, remember?

Kirsty (*grumpy, giving in*) Oh all right. (*She exits through the back.*)

Sabrina (*musing aloud*) I'm trying to think how to best explain it. There's a world of difference between you and me. Yes, though we all come from the great source of creativity, some of us, well, how can I put it without seeming to be judgemental, are more elegantly made, some of us rather more roughly cut. It isn't your fault at all that you've all been badly written.

Neil Ow. Oow. She's doing it again.

Iona Doing what again?

Neil Suggesting that we're imaginary. Oh, my head.

Iona It's very impolite of her.

Sabrina I honestly mean no offence. But you've been implicated in a structure that, well, excuse me for saying it, has no theatrical merit, at least not as far as I can make out.

Neil I miss the old days, Iona. When things were straightforward. When it was just you and me here, just a boy and a girl. When we would argue amicably about nothing every night till the dark came, then we would go to bed, and get up next morning and it would be breakfast time, right now, it would be breakfast time, and just us here, no one else telling us who we are and who we're not, just us sitting quietly at the breakfast table having breakfast, by ourselves.

Kirsty (*entering, with water*) I'm back! What have I missed?

Iona Thank you, Kirsty. Your friend was just telling us the difference between her and us.

Sabrina It's not that you're imaginary, exactly. The fact is, you exist on a different plane.

Kirsty Like an aeroplane?

Sabrina I'm not being exclusive. There's room in the universe for all the different planes of existence. And we can visit many of them. We ought to visit as many as possible. It is mind-expanding.

Kirsty You have to face the facts, you two. Sabrina is a special visitor come from another place to tell you these truths. You ought to listen to her. If she thinks you should take a plane somewhere, then you definitely should. I'll look after the flat while you're away. I won't have any parties or anything, I promise.

Sabrina And it is one of the most important things to do, to admit the truth. Especially about our identity. I taught an evening class on this subject last year. It's terribly important to understand our constructed selves. It's terribly important to deconstruct ourselves, to tear ourselves apart.

Neil Oh, my stomach.

Sabrina To rip through our misconceptions and throw them away. Come on now, rip them up.

Iona Mine's beginning to hurt too. Maybe we ate something.

Kirsty Mine's fine. Probably because I never actually got anything to eat.

Sabrina This will help us understand how we exist. And the truth is, when it comes to you, 'exist' is a relative term. Being just characters.

Kirsty Yeah. See, this is your problem. You and Neil, you're both just characters.

Sabrina (*to Kirsty*) Well, but you're a character too.

Kirsty (*jaw dropping*) *I'm* –? Ow! My stomach!

Sabrina And you're all caricatures. I am the only one here on the stage who is really real. For instance, if I was a character in this play, like all of you, then I would probably also have been very badly drawn. And I'm hardly a caricature of an awful English incomer. Am I?

Kirsty She says I'm not real! Ow! My head! Not real! My stomach! What a fucking nerve!

Sabrina Do you remember the discussion we had about swearing back in the first act?

Kirsty Fuck! Ow! Shit!

Sabrina Your swearing is only creating terrible karma for yourself and your friends.

Kirsty I'm just as fucking bloody well real as you!

Sabrina Is that why you do it? To make yourself feel more authentic?

Iona And we are, too, just as fucking bloody well real, aren't we, Neil?

Neil I don't know any more. Am I a man? Am I a woman? Do the Hendersons exist?

Iona Oh. The Hendersons. I'd forgotten all about them.

Neil Is there breakfast? Is there a world? Is there a God?

Iona (*gets the salt-and-pepper grinder, puts it squarely in front of Neil*) I *know* there is. (*And now to Sabrina, making the effort for the both of them.*) We're really real, too. Aren't we, Kirsty?

Kirsty (*teamwork*) Yes. We're all real here. (*She points at Sabrina.*) Except her. She's the only one who's not real here. (*to Sabrina*) You're not real. How's your stomach?

Sabrina Revelation is painful. I know. But being dispossessed of illusion is liberating. Feel it! Feel the freedom!

Neil Ow.

Iona Ow.

Kirsty Ow!

Sabrina If we all join together, sit on the floor, gather in a circle and close our eyes, I'll lead us in a meditation which will help everyone relax a bit.

Neil Will it make us any more real?

Sabrina Transcendental meditation can take you into a different world.

Neil I don't want to go to a different world. I want to go back to the old world.

Sabrina I'm obviously here for a reason. I've obviously been sent to help you all. We will achieve harmony together. This is a very conflicted place. I can feel it. There are vibes, everywhere. Brrr. (*Shakes her hands, as if to shake out bad vibes.*) There is such a history of *drama* on this stage. No wonder you're all upset with each other.

Kirsty We're not upset with each other. We're upset with *you*. It's you that's upset our stomachs.

Sabrina I'd like to take this place and make it into a New Age centre. This town needs one. Plays as uncouth and anti-dramatic as this are a waste of sacred theatrical space. Plays as formless and different as this one should be stopped. They should be done away with.

Kirsty Miss Cleverclogs. Miss Realer-than-thou.

Sabrina I will not leave this play until I've done a full purification ritual.

Kirsty I've a good mind to punch you a good one.

Sabrina No violence, please. Violence is the most reactionary reaction. It is juvenile. It is common and Neanderthal.

Kirsty Good and hard, right on the nose. Show you how really real I am.

Iona Stop it, Kirsty. You're only making her more determined not to leave.

Kirsty starts trying to push Sabrina off the stage. Sabrina fights back.

Kirsty Scared your weirdo friends 'out there' 'll see you getting beaten up by someone who's not real, eh? Eh?

Sabrina (*struggling*) You cannot force me against my will. I call for more understanding for these minds. I call for more listening, for the floodgate of understanding to open. I am a pacifist. I abhor violence. The only thing in the world I abhor more than I abhor violence is karaoke.

Kirsty (*stops pushing*) Is what?

Sabrina The pub next to where I live has a karaoke three times a week. I loathe it.

Kirsty Why? What is it?

Sabrina It is reactionary, juvenile, common and Neanderthal.

Iona Just like violence?

Sabrina Quiet, everybody. I am about to begin a special spirit-blessing and exorcism.

She calmly pushes Kirsty out of the way and gets up onto the table. Sits on it in the meditating position. Starts meditating. Is immediately oblivious. Unearthly

69

*silence. Everything pauses. Neil has his eyes tight shut.
Iona stands up, rubbing her hands on her sides.*

Kirsty What's karaoke? (*to audience*) What is it?

Iona Kirsty. Don't bring any more of these friends of
yours in here. Can't you see the state Neil's in?

Neil No Neil. No Iona. No Hendersons.

Iona No more of them, Kirsty.

She takes Kirsty aside, whispering.

I'm afraid for him. I think if one more thing happens it'll
be – the straw that breaks the camel's back.

Kirsty (*whispering*) What's karaoke? I need to know.

Iona Kirsty. You brought your friend here. It was nice of
you, and it was nice of her to visit, and Neil and I enjoyed
her company. We were hospitable, weren't we? We offered
her food without a face, and everything. But now – and
I'm asking you this as a sister –

Kirsty (*surprisingly moved*) Oh. As a sister? A real sister?

Iona Uh huh.

Kirsty As if I was actually possibly in real life really your
sister?

Iona Yes. It's just a small thing. But can you maybe
arrange for your friend to leave? Because it's early, Kirsty,
and I have to get everything back to normal. I think Neil
and I would really appreciate having breakfast in peace.
We both have to get off to work in about half an hour,
and we've had no sleep all night, what with all the
excitement.

Kirsty Let me get this straight. You want *her* to go.

Iona That's it.

Kirsty But you don't want *me* to go.

Neil groans.

Iona That's right.

Kirsty And then after she goes . . . I can maybe stay on . . . as your . . . sister?

Neil groans.

Iona Yes, that's possible.

Kirsty Even though . . . you know . . . I'm *not* it.

Neil groans.

Iona Uh huh.

Kirsty Does he agree about this?

Neil groans.

Iona (*nudging Neil to be quiet*) He agrees. Just – Kirsty – be a love. Find some way of asking your friend to go back where she came from. And Kirsty – whatever happens. No more people coming in through the wall. Okay? Right?

Kirsty Right. Okay. (*Pacing, thinking.*) I'll sort it. I'll get her out of here. Ah! I know what to do. Look after my things. I'm just going out now, for a short walk in the snow. I may be some time. (*Exits at front door.*)

Neil (*daring to open his eyes*) It's so quiet. Are they gone?

Iona One of our guests is still with us.

Neil Where's the other one gone?

Iona I don't know. How about I make us some breakfast at long last? I could make us a lovely breakfast.

Neil But *she*'s on the table.

Iona That's okay. We can do that ignoring thing again. Do you want to try? How are you feeling?

Neil (*making effort*) Okay. Okay, I'll try. Because things are nearly back to normal, aren't they?

Iona That's right.

Neil No more being invaded by them?

Iona That's right, love.

Neil I don't think I could bear another invasion.

Iona Just us, not them. I promise. Now. What would you like for breakfast? I'll make you anything you want. Anything you want in the world.

Neil I think I'd just like ordinary breakfast today, please. The kind of breakfast we have on an ordinary normal kind of day.

Iona My pleasure.

Iona starts laying the table for breakfast round Sabrina, who's still sitting on it in a trance. She exits at the back, comes back, humming a tune as if in domestic bliss, with plates and bread and cereal.

Iona One egg or two?

Neil My stomach's still a bit funny-feeling. I'll just have toast, if that's okay.

Iona Anything you want, love. Coffee or tea?

Neil Coffee. With sugar in it.

Iona I know. You like it sweet.

Iona exits, and we can hear her through the back, clattering pans about. Neil is slowly getting calmer, coming back to his old self. He stands up. He stretches. He looks around. He regains some of his old bearing.

He goes up to Sabrina, gets close to her, bravely. He waves his hand in front of her face. He pokes her with his finger. She doesn't register anything.

Neil Think you could scare me, did you? Huh. Didn't scare me. Couldn't scare me. Not in my own house. At my own breakfast table. Well, I'm going to sit right here, ghost. And I'm going to eat my toast right in front of – (*He is suddenly struck by a thought.*) Iona?

Iona (*through the back*) Yes, love?

Neil What kind of bread is it that you're making toast with?

Iona (*through the back*) The kind you like, honest.

Neil (*stricken*) Oh no! What if it's ciabatta?

Neil goes through to check. When he leaves the stage, there's just Sabrina on it, still meditating.
    Now, down to the front of the stage, out of the audience, creeps Janice, out of the seat that was kept for her, and as if it's been her first chance to come down and do this. She gets to the edge and tries to attract Sabrina's attention.

Janice Pssst. Sabrina. Psssst. (*A little louder.*) Sabrina! What are you doing? Get off the stage! (*Louder.*) *Sabrina!*

She's got her umbrella with her. She presses the telescoping bit out, and tries to reach and nudge Sabrina with it, but it's too short. There's nothing else for it. She has to get up onto the stage. So she does.

Sabrina, come *on*. I know it's supposed to be experimental and everything, but you're holding up the play. Oh no. Oh God. (*She lifts up one of Sabrina's eyelids carefully.*) The last time she was like this it took four days for her to come round. Sabrina. For the love of God, Sabrina, come on. There's people. Watching. They've paid money.

73

Janice gives up. She starts looking round the flat. She appraises the furnishings, the bits and pieces, picks them up, puts them down, wondering what everything's worth. She sees the salt-and-pepper grinder, picks it up.

Quite nice.

Iona comes through with a coffee pot and two cups on saucers piled on each other. She sees Janice. She drops the cups. Janice jumps.

Oh for God's sake! What a fright you gave me!

Neil (*still through the back*) Iona? Are you all right?

Iona Yes, love! Fine, love! Everything's fine! Don't come through!

Janice I was just –

Iona Where are you from?

Janice Eh?

Iona *Where* are you *from*?

Janice Well, originally I was born in Nairn, my dad had a kilt shop there, we lived near the beach and everything. I used to love it. Funny how being in front of an audience makes you want to talk! Once I remember, when I was really small, we were feeding some ponies in a field and we saw Charlie Chaplin. You know, the old movie star. Apparently he used to like coming to Nairn for his holidays. He didn't have his moustache or his hat or anything, he just looked like an old man. My mum said, 'Look, that's Charlie Chaplin.' But it just looked like an old man. He didn't even look rich. That's amazing, that, eh? But it *was* him. But I haven't lived there for years. For the past fifteen years I've been living in ———— (*name of nearby place*).

74

Iona (*speechless for a moment, then*) Did you come through the door or did you come through the wall?

Janice Sorry?

Iona The door or the wall? The door or the wall?

Janice I just got here. I've only been here for ten minutes, since the beginning of the second act.

Iona Oh no!

Janice I missed the first act, and when I got here she wasn't in her seat or anything, and then the play started up and I was sitting in my seat and I couldn't believe my eyes, there she was on the stage!

Iona (*sinking to the floor, defeated*) You're one of *them*.

Janice Eh, what do you mean by that, exactly?

Iona It's terrible. It's the last straw. I really honestly don't know what to do any more.

Janice Has she ruined it? We went to see *Hamlet* last week, and I could feel she was sitting beside me on the edge of her seat itching to shout out in the middle of it. I get it all the way home. 'I once saw Glenda Jackson do Medea, these groups up here can't be expected to be as good as that.' We've got nothing in common. We're so different. I don't really know why we're friends, except that she pays me to fix – uh, do the accounts for her evening classes. Oh well. (*She crouches down beside Iona.*) Tell me something. I've always wanted to know. Is there money in acting? No? I didn't think so. What kind of a play was this, anyway? I couldn't make it out.

Iona Neil is going to die.

Janice Oh God. A tragedy. I hate tragedies. What a bore. Someone always has to die.

75

Iona No, I mean Neil is going to die if he sees you here. He will die. He will see you, see you're one of them, and it will be the end. And my life, at least as I've known it, will be over too.

Janice Oh. I'm awful sorry. I was only trying to help. Look – here. Here you go.

She picks up the cups and saucers, gives them to Iona.

Only, see, the thing is, the last time she was like this. This is why my alarm bells went off when I saw her on the stage. She was meditating. On top of a Mini Metro van. It was a protest about air pollution. She slewed the van across the middle of the road outside Marks and Spencer's in Inverness, threw the keys down a drain and sat on the bonnet and wouldn't move. It took two policemen and a tow-truck to lift her.

Neil (*coming through*) To lift who?

Iona Oh no. Oh God. (*She jumps to her feet.*) Neil! Uh, uh – darling! Guess! Guess who this is! No! You'll never guess. This is, uh, this is – this is –

Janice Janice.

Iona Janice – H-Henderson!

Janice Eh . . .?

Iona Mrs Janice A. Henderson! From the flat across the hall!

Neil (*brightening remarkably*) Mrs Henderson! Really? Really! Well well! My goodness! (*shaking her hand*) I can't tell you how pleased I am to meet you, Mrs Henderson.

Janice Oh, just call me Janice.

Iona Mrs Henderson, I mean Janice, is just back from her holidays, Neil.

76

Neil Is that right? Where is it you were, Janice?

Iona Oh, she went to, what was it, Nairn. It was a beach holiday, wasn't it Janice?

Janice Em, eh –

Neil And how long for?

Iona Fifteen ye— uh, days, wasn't it, Janice? Oh, she had a great time, didn't you? She saw horses, and a man who looked remarkably unlike Charlie Chaplin, and she was wearing a kilt and everything, and she's been telling me all about all the sights she saw. And how she saw a, a – an elephant at the circus, and it needed, what was it, a tow-truck, and two policemen, to lift it off the ground. For some reason.

Neil Well! Sounds like you had a lovely time.

Janice I was just leaving, actually –

Neil Oh no, don't go yet! It's such a pleasure to meet you at last, Janice. Do you know, for a wee while there we actually thought that because we'd never met you, you might not exist!

Janice Look, eh, I'm sorry, but I'm not –

Neil (*still shaking Janice's hand*) I can't tell you what it means to meet you in person, in the flesh. It – it means the world to me.

Iona And I was just telling Janice, Neil, that you've been a little off-colour for the last day or so, that you've not been feeling yourself, and that just when the both of us felt like we might really need and appreciate the support of our neighbours, just for the next wee while, not long, just while we're seeing ourselves out of what's been quite a rough patch, just like a miracle there was a knock on the front door, not the wall, and I opened it, the door,

77

and this lady, this one here, in front of us, said, 'Hello, my name is Mrs Janice Henderson and I live across the hall from you and I was wondering if you'd any spare, uh . . . salt you could let me have?' Isn't that right, eh, Janice?

Janice Oh yes. Uh huh. That's right. I was needing salt. For my – uh – porridge.

Neil So you like a traditional breakfast, do you, Janice?

Janice (*lost*) Oh yes, uh huh, nothing better.

Iona Oh yes. I can tell we'll all soon be old friends can't you?

Janice And I was wondering if my neighbours could maybe lend me a few quid, just till I get to the bank? I mislaid my card, it got eaten, you know, by the machine, and I just need a tenner, or maybe twenty pounds, to get me through the day till I sort it out . . .?

Iona (*nodding*) Oh yes, no problem. I'll find my purse. I think I can even lend you fifty, if you'd like that.

Janice Oh yes, fifty sounds about right, let's make it fifty.

Iona It'd be terrible to find yourself short.

Janice Oh, it would. Anything you say. I'll, eh, pop across the hall later and give it back to you. Directly after I've been to the bank.

Iona But not before you've had a chat with us about yourself, your life as a member of the Henderson family and everything.

Janice Exactly. Anything you say.

Neil But where's your husband, Janice? Will we get to meet him too? I could do with some male company about the place. He'll know exactly what I mean.

Janice Oh, I don't have a husband.

Iona (*overlapping*) He works abroad.

Neil Sorry?

Janice He works abroad.

Iona (*overlapping*) He's dead.

Neil Oh! Oh that's terrible. I'm so sorry to hear that. When did this happen?

Janice It was a tragedy.

Iona He was working abroad when it happened.

Neil (*mortified*) I'm so sorry –

Janice No no, never mind. It feels like a whole other life to me.

Neil I'm glad.

Iona You've got to get over these things, haven't you Janice, and on with your new life.

Janice Oh yes. I feel like I don't even know her at all, the person I must have been supposed to be being, back then.

Neil Right. That's all to the good, isn't it? Life moves on.

Janice At a dizzying rate.

Iona Well, who's for some coffee?

Neil Coffee, Janice?

Janice Oh no thanks, not for me.

Iona Oh. Oh well.

Janice You don't have any tea, do you?

Iona (*keen, almost excited*) Tea? You'd like me to make you a cup of tea? (*suddenly thwarted*) Ah – but you probably want a special kind of tea.

Janice Oh no, any old plain old tea please.

Iona Really? Really?

Janice Just a bag in a cup, that'd be lovely.

Iona I'll get you a cup of tea!

Janice As long as it's wet and brown that'll suit me down to the ground.

Iona (*delighted, off through the back*) I'll put the kettle on! Oh Janice, it's so lovely that you're here!

Janice (*pleased*) Thank you. That's awful nice.

Neil Sit down, Janice, have a seat – eh – (*He turns to the table, which has Sabrina sitting up on it.*) Oh. This is, em, em – (*He can't think how to explain her, so he says:*) – Iona's sister, Kirsty.

Janice Is it?

Neil Yes. Her little sister. She's just passing through. She's doing, eh – um – Iona?

Iona (*coming back through*) Yes, love?

Neil What is it again, that Kirsty's doing?

Iona Oh. Kirsty's my little sister, Janice. Well, not really my little sister, but, you know. She's wonderful. She used to work at a circus and she can read minds and she told us the story about the seer, do you know about the seer? He was born here, in our building. She'll be back in a minute. She's going to tell me some more things about him. It's completely fascinating. She's just nipped out to help us get rid of –

Neil No, no, *this* Kirsty. What is it that *this* Kirsty, your little sister here, on the table, is doing up on the table like that?

Iona Oh. Oh. This Kirsty. You mean *Kirsty* Kirsty. My other little sister. My mother was, um, very fond of the name Kirsty.

Janice Yes, she must have been.

Iona Oh, she was.

Janice That's kind of like the Gaelic, isn't it, Kirsty-Kirsty?

Iona I've got an older sister called Kirsty too. Haven't I, Neil?

Neil Oh yes. She was born first.

Iona We used to call her, um –

Neil Firsty Kirsty.

Janice It must have been confusing in your house when she called you all in for your supper.

Iona Oh yes. It was all 'Kirsty! Kirsty-Kirsty! Firsty Kirsty! Iona!'

Janice And this one here is Kirsty-Kirsty?

Iona We call her Kirsty for short. She's, she's – doing a sponsored sleep.

Janice Oh. For charity?

Neil Yes. I mean, no.

Iona (*overlapping*) No. I mean, yes.

Janice That's great. That's an easy way to make money, eh? I could do that all day.

Iona Ha ha! I'll just fetch that tea, Janice.

Janice And your purse? Don't forget.

Iona I won't! I won't be a minute. (*She exits at back.*)

Neil Have a seat. Don't mind, eh, Kirsty. Eh, I mean, Kirsty-Kirsty.

Janice Thank you.

Neil So what is it that the mysterious Mrs Henderson from across the hall does for a living?

Janice I don't know. I don't know her.

Neil What d'you mean –?

Janice Oh, me! I'm sorry, I forgot who I was for a minute. Now. What do I do for a living? I sell used cars for cash.

Neil (*distaste*) Oh.

Janice Are you interested in a car? I could get you any model you like. I'll even let you name your price. You won't get a better deal. Since we're friends and neighbours and all.

Neil Oh no. Thank you.

Janice What is it *you* do for a living?

Neil Oh I couldn't possibly tell you that. It's confidential.

Janice But I told *you*!

Neil Yes, but what you do clearly isn't confidential or vital for the formation of contemporary national identity.

Janice You smug bastard!

Neil Please don't swear. It isn't becoming in a woman.

Janice Don't start with that shit! I get it enough of the time from her –

Neil From who?

Janice Uh, nobody. Nothing. Anyway, how do you know? How do you know that what I do isn't confidential or vital or important enough or whatever it was you said?

Neil You just told me yourself! You sell used cars!

Janice How do you know I'm not making that up?

Neil Why else would you have said it?

Iona (*entering at back*) Here's a lovely cup of tea, Janice.

Janice Your husband's an oaf. He's a snob. That's it. I'm not playing this game a moment longer.

Iona He's not my husband. Neil, what have you done now?

Neil I merely said what I believe.

Janice What you believe?!

Neil I am a truthful man. I pride myself on my honesty. I never lie about things.

Janice You never lie? Is that so? You never lie?

Iona Oh, no . . .

Neil Never.

Janice (*pointing at Sabrina*) Then who's this? Tell me! Tell me who this is! Tell me her name!

Iona (*everything is crumbling. She holds out the cup*) Oh, oh dear. Janice. Here. Drink your tea.

Janice Her name.

Neil (*trying to loosen his collar with his finger*) Her name. I . . . uh . . . it's –

Janice Remember – you never tell a lie.

Neil This is – her name is –

> *The front door flies open. Enter Kirsty at a run. She heads straight for her rucksack.*

Iona (*relieved – change of subject*) Kirsty! You're home!

Neil (*relieved to be out of it*) Kirsty! Welcome back, Kirsty!

Kirsty is opening her rucksack. She roots about inside it, throwing handfuls of paper money out behind her all over the floor. Soon the floor is covered in cash.

Kirsty Don't interrupt me! Don't say anything! I've found the solution! It's only going to cost me the hire of the karaoke machine. There's a guy waiting down the stairs in a van. I've just got to pay him this much and we can get rid of her and everything will be all right and I can be your actual real sister again and stay for ages and ages –

Kirsty stands up, turns round with a fistful of money. Sees Janice. Her eyes widen. Her jaw drops. She drops the money. She has fallen completely in love.

Who is that beautiful apparition passing before me?

Janice (*kneeling down*) This money looks awful real.

Kirsty She's – the most beautiful creature I have ever seen!

Janice It feels real. Is this, like, play-money? It's incredibly realistic if it is.

Kirsty Who is she?

Iona Kirsty, this is Janice Henderson.

Kirsty Janice Henderson! What a beautiful name!

Neil From *across* the *hall*.

Kirsty A name conjured by angels!

Neil (*mimics Kirsty*) What if the Hendersons don't exist, what if the Hendersons are a figment of your imagination?

Kirsty Are you real? Do you exist? Am I making you up?

Neil They exist. And now we've met one, and we all exist.

Kirsty Such beauty, such perfection, can't be real.

Janice There's thousands of pounds here. I'm sure it's real.

Kirsty And here you are, the real thing!

Iona Janice, this is –

Janice (*fingering the money, ignoring them*) Yeah yeah, I know. Kirsty.

Kirsty Your first words to me. The way you said my name! I can hardly speak!

Janice Whatever.

Iona What's the matter with Kirsty?

Neil I *knew* there was something funny about her.

Kirsty (*to Janice*) I can hardly breathe! My heart! It's going like mad! I can't believe this is happening!

Janice That's nice.

Kirsty 'That's nice.' What a beautiful thing to say. She's divine!

Janice Uh huh.

Kirsty I feel like I could say *anything* to you.

Neil I knew there was something funny about *her*, too.

Iona Neil. That's enough.

Kirsty (*eyes only for Janice, in amazement*) I feel like I could *be* anyone. I've never felt like this before. I feel all pure. I feel all new.

Janice (*still in distracted wonder at all the money*) Good. Good for you.

Kirsty I feel all . . . possible again.

Awkward pause on stage, as Janice tries to figure out how to pocket the money without being seen, while Kirsty stares at her, stunned, Sabrina carries on meditating and Neil and Iona wait – Neil bored and huffy, Iona calm – as if for something to happen. Then Iona takes gentle charge.

Iona Kirsty.

Kirsty (*amazed*) I'm in love.

Iona Yes. It's lovely. I'm so pleased for you. And as your sister I'll stand by any unorthodox decisions you make in your love life with all my heart.

Neil *I* won't.

Iona Be quiet, Neil.

Kirsty You're both being unbelievably patronising.

Iona (*to Kirsty*) But what was it that you came rushing in here a couple of minutes ago in such a hurry for again?

Kirsty (*coming to her senses*) I don't remember. That was in my other life. Before everything changed.

Iona Try, Kirsty. Otherwise nothing's going to happen for ages and Neil and I have got to get to work *some* time this morning.

Kirsty Wait – that's right. I remember. I have to pay a man in a van. It'll only take a second. (*to Janice*) Please don't go anywhere. Don't disappear. Please. I'll be right back.

She takes a handful of the money, counts it quickly and exits out the front door, slamming it behind her.

Neil Janice. Regardless of the disagreements we've had, I feel it's only fair I make it clear to you that the money you're putting in your pockets was most probably come by unlawfully.

Janice So?

Neil I wouldn't touch it if I were you.

Janice You're not me.

Iona Janice, that money's not yours to take.

Janice Yes, but you don't mind me taking it, do you? Since I'm your neighbour and my second name's Henderson and all?

Neil She's unscrupulous.

Iona (*mournfully*) She is. You're right.

Janice (*standing up*) Well, nearly time for me to go. Back to my 'flat'. Lovely meeting you both.

She shakes their hands, even though both her hands are full of money.

Iona So soon? Don't you want this cup of tea?

Janice No, no thank you. I've just remembered an urgent business meeting I really must attend. Now. All that remains to sort out is that little matter of fifty pounds we agreed about earlier.

Iona I think you've plenty there to keep you going.

Janice Listen. We made a neighbourly deal.

Iona Neil, will you fetch a cup of salt from the kitchen for Mrs Henderson?

Neil Why do I have to do it?

Iona Neil.

Exit Neil by the back.

Iona Don't mess with me, Janice whoever-you-are. This isn't your world. You don't know the rules here.

Janice What's this? The worm turning?

Iona (*getting more and more threatening*) You came in here uninvited. I welcomed you, offered you money, even made you a cup of tea. And you didn't drink it.

Janice (*unsettled*) So? There's no law against that, is there?

Iona Too many people have been turning down my tea, Janice. Let's be more precise. One too many people has turned down my tea. And it's you, Janice. You. You've made me angry. It's not something that happens often. But when it happens . . . I ought to warn you, Janice. This is the house where Finn MacFinn MacFinn MacFinn the great and legendary seer was born.

Janice Yeah yeah.

Iona And the powers of the house pass down the line to those who live here.

Janice Sure they do. We said fifty quid. I'm not budging.

Iona The curse of the seer, Janice, isn't something to be blasé about.

Janice A curse? Yeah yeah. Ha ha.

Iona And I can curse you, Janice, if I choose, so succinctly that when you leave this room through that wall any second now, if I want it to, the money in your hands will turn to honey, the cash in your pockets will turn to ash.

Janice Will what?

Iona And all your dealings with money, Janice, from this moment on, will be sticky.

Janice Oh all right then, all right then, give me the bloody cup, I'll drink it now.

Iona And bitter.

Janice I'm drinking it. I'm going. I'm going. Okay?

Iona You'd better go, Janice, before the words of the curse rise to my mouth.

Janice What kind of a play is this? You can't order an audience around like that! I'm going to write to the people who gave you your grant and ask them to revoke it. This play'll never tour.

Iona I'm warning you Janice, for the last time. Here they come, the words of the curse, I can feel them, rising –

Janice Okay okay, I'm going, for God's sake.

Janice jumps off the stage. She turns and puts the cup and the saucer back on it, and then she's off, into the dark of the theatre, and out of the theatre.

Iona There. That was great. I really enjoyed it. (*She picks up the cup and saucer. Pleased with herself. Her old self again.*) Drank all her tea!

Neil (*entering at back with a cup*) Where's she gone?

Iona Back to her flat.

Neil (*putting the cup of salt on the table, next to Sabrina's foot*) She forgot her cup of salt. I didn't hear the door.

Iona No, she was quiet as a mouse.

Neil Thank God she left us some of the money. Well, we're rich. At last.

Iona This is Kirsty's money, Neil, not ours.

Neil Yes, but since she'll surely be up for splitting it with us. Fifty-fifty. Sixty-forty at least. Since she's a wanted felon. And your sister, and everything.

Iona You've changed your tune.

Neil You'll talk to her about it, won't you?

Iona It's hers.

Neil Please?

Iona No.

Neil Maybe she'll never come back. Then we'll just inherit it. We could do anything with this. We could buy anything. We could buy a better house.

Iona *Neil*. That's enough. It's not ours. It's not yours.

Short huffy, annoyed silence. Then:

Neil There's something really dodgy about that Janice Henderson, Iona.

Iona Takes all kinds.

Neil Maybe losing her husband has unhinged her.

Iona Anything's possible.

Neil I think she was lying about something. I feel it in my bones.

Iona No doubt.

Neil Iona, I think we should maybe move. I don't know if I want to live next to such insalubrious neighbours.

Iona Oh no. I'm never moving. I like living here. I like this house. It's full of possibilities. It is the birthplace of the seer.

Neil Iona, love. I don't want to hear you going on about any of that nonsense any more.

Iona You don't know. You don't understand how powerful it is.

Neil I don't want to hear another word about it. It's lies. How many times do I have to tell you? There's no seer. There never was a seer. She made it all up. It's made up.

Iona It isn't, Neil.

Neil It is.

Iona It isn't.

Neil It *is*.

Iona *Isn't!*

Neil *Is!*

Iona (*outburst*) All sorts of things aren't automatically not true just because you want them not to be. Things don't stop being true just because you think they're not!

Neil Em . . .

Iona You make me so mad! You wouldn't believe me about the music! You never let me hear what I hear! You never let me see what I see! You never let me believe what I want to believe!

Neil That's because you always want to believe in such rubbish.

Iona You never let me believe what I *need* to believe!

Neil You're completely unsuited for survival. If it wasn't for me, you'd never survive.

Iona What do you mean? What do you mean by that?

Neil You can't even make a sane decision on your own.

Iona You're cruel. And heartless. And selfish. And sexist. And slight. They were right.

Neil You always capitulate. You never use your brain.

Iona And rude.

Neil Sometimes I wonder if you've got a brain in there.

Iona And arrogant.

Neil Hello? Calling Iona's brain!

Iona And horrible.

Neil No answer.

Iona And poisonous.

Neil Empty, like I thought.

Iona Just shut up, Neil!

Neil You'd die without me.

Iona I'd die without you? I hate you! The only way I'll ever get to *live* is if I'm without you!

> *Iona slams out of the front door. Neil watches her, shocked, then marches through the back and slams a door through there. Short hostile silence, clear stage. Then Sabrina takes a deep breath in and opens her eyes.*

Sabrina Have I brought about harmony, peace and serenity? (*Looks around her, sees all the money strewn all over the floor.*) That's never happened before! I'll have to try this again, at home. (*She reaches down, serenely picks up the cup at her feet and tries to drink from it, spits salt out.*) Bleagh! Yuch! Ugh! (*She wipes her mouth. Regains composure.*) My work is done here. (*to audience*) If any of you would like me to come and do the same as you've seen me do here in your own home, or even in the workplace, I have special rates. Speak to me after the play, or call my mobile and leave me a message on 078 888 123 45. That's 078 888 123 45.

> *Sabrina is getting off the stage, going back to her seat, just as Kirsty comes in backwards at the front door, dragging behind her a machine and speakers and a giant screen, on a trolley. She sees Sabrina leaving. She kicks the door shut.*

Kirsty (*looking at machine*) Wow. That worked pretty well, then.

Neil comes through from the back, thinking it must have been Iona at the door. When he sees Kirsty he looks disappointed. Kirsty is preoccupied too, wondering where Janice has gone.

Kirsty Where's –?

Neil Where's –?

Kirsty Where did Janice go?

Neil Have you seen Iona?

Kirsty goes straight back out of the front door. Sound of knocking. No answer. Neil realises that Sabrina has left. He looks at the money. Without Iona, he doesn't care about it. He looks bereft. Kirsty comes back in, also looking bereft.

Kirsty Maybe she'll be back in later.

Neil What's this?

Kirsty It's a machine that ghosts are frightened of.

Neil What does it do?

Kirsty It doesn't do anything. All I had to do was bring it into the room, and she ran away. (*She reads from the instruction manual.*) 'Plug it in, select your Scottish song, press the number, and the words will appear on the screen, then just sing along to the tune in the good old time-honoured way!'

Neil (*looking at the wall*) Are they . . . are they still out there?

Kirsty (*squinting out at the audience*) Yep. But who cares about them? Who cares about the other world when this world is so transformed, so different, so full of life, and love, and Janice Henderson?

*Front door opens. Iona comes in. She won't look at
Neil. Neil is pleased and relieved she's back, but
immediately moody and angry again. He won't look
at her either.*

Kirsty What's the matter with you two?

Iona Nothing.

Neil Nothing.

Kirsty Sure?

Neil Absolutely nothing's the matter with me.

Iona Or me.

Neil I'm absolutely fine.

Iona Me too. I'm absolutely fine too.

Kirsty Eh . . . good. I'm fine too. (*Short silence.*) Well.
What'll we do while we wait for Janice to come back to
her flat? Will we have breakfast?

Iona I'm not hungry.

Neil Nor me.

Kirsty Will we play a game of Monopoly?

Iona sighs. Neil sighs.

Kirsty Oh. Oh well, then. (*Short silence. Then:*) How
long do you think it'll be before Janice comes back to her
flat? (*Short silence.*) D'you think it'll be long? (*Short
silence.*) D'you think Janice liked me? (*Short silence.*)
I wonder what Janice's favourite colour is. (*Short silence.*)
How long do you think it'll be before Janice comes back
to her flat?

Iona Kirsty. There's something you ought to know. And
it's this. Janice didn't go back to any flat.

Kirsty Didn't go back to –? But where did she go, then?

Iona Janice is a –

Kirsty A what?

Iona She's from –

Kirsty From where?

Iona She isn't one of – (*She's about to say 'one of us' but, still out of deference to Neil, she won't, can't, say it.*) I don't think Janice is really a good idea for you, Kirsty.

Kirsty What are you saying? Where did Janice go if she didn't go back to the flat? She could be anywhere. Anywhere in the world!

Iona She didn't seem at all like a nice person.

Kirsty Not a nice person! Janice Henderson! How can you say that! Where did she go? Where? Where? You have to tell me!

Iona (*deference*) To the bank. She – she went to the bank.

Kirsty Oh. Right. (*Short silence.*) Do you think it'll be long before she's back from the bank?

Iona sighs. Neil sighs. It dawns on Kirsty finally that they're both really miserable, that they've had a fight. She thinks. She wonders what to do. She has an idea.

(*reading list of songs on the karaoke machine*) 'Scots Wha Hae. Loch Lomond. Skye Boat Song. Westering Home. Annie Laurie. Ae Fond Kiss. Lewis Bridal Song. Bonnie Lass o' Fyvie. Wild Mountain Thyme . . .'

Iona (*enthusiastic*) Oh – I like that one. That's my favourite. (*Then remembers she's sulking.*)

Kirsty plugs in the karaoke. It lights up. She presses a number. Music starts playing, the music for 'Wild

Mountain Thyme'. It sounds remarkably like the music playing at the start of the play. The words come up on the screen, nobody singing them.

OH THE SUMMER TIME HAS COME
AND THE TREES ARE SWEETLY BLOOMIN
THE WILD MOUNTAIN THYME
GROWS AROUND THE BLOOMIN HEATHER
WILL YE GO LASSIE GO
AND WE'LL ALL GO TOGETHER
TO PULL WILD MOUNTAIN THYME
ALL AROUND THE BLOOMIN HEATHER
WILL YE GO LASSIE GO.

While this is playing, Kirsty gets the microphone. She gives it to Neil. She suggests, without saying anything, that he sing the song to Iona. Neil at first is reluctant. Then shy. Then he sings, shyly, movingly amateurishly, these words to her:

Neil
I will build my love a bower
By a cool crystal fountain
And round it I will pile
All the wild flowers of the mountain.

Iona (*moved*) Oh! Oh, Neil. I don't think I ever heard you sing before.

Neil That's because I can't, not really. I wish I could. I wish I could sing better for you.

Iona You can! That's so beautiful!

Neil I'd sing you such beautiful songs if I could.

Iona You sang perfectly. That was the loveliest song I've ever had sung to me.

Neil (*pleased*) Was it?

Iona Ever in my whole life.

96

Neil Aw. Love.

Iona That was just lovely, love.

Neil I'm sorry.

Iona Aw, Neil. I'm sorry too.

Neil No, I'm sorry. It was my fault.

Iona No, no, I was to blame.

> *Kirsty pulls the plug out of the karaoke machine – the lights stopping, words disappearing, music stopping all at once.*

Kirsty That's you two sorted. Now can we talk about me again?

Iona The old songs are the best.

Kirsty Depending on their adaptability to new ways of singing them.

Neil There's a bottle of champagne in the fridge, isn't there?

Iona I think so.

Neil (*about to go and get it, turning to speak to Kirsty*) Kirsty, you're very welcome to stay.

Kirsty That's just as well, since I'm staying.

Neil No, I mean – Kirsty. You're very welcome.

> *Neil exits through the back. Kirsty makes a face at Iona.*

Kirsty Well, that only took several hours and an almost all-out war and a karaoke machine.

Iona No, but it's true, Kirsty. You are welcome to stay here. As long as you want. We're family now. You're family.

Kirsty How can plants bear to stay bulbs below the ground in a world with Janice Henderson on the surface?

Iona There's something I have to tell you, though, Kirsty.

Kirsty How can the sun bear to go down at night in such a world, how can the moon bear to give way to the sun again the next morning?

Iona The thing is, Kirsty –

Kirsty The world is wonderful, full of wonder. To put it simply, I once was lost but now I'm found.

Iona The thing is. This is awful hard to say, Kirsty, believe me. But –

> *There's a brisk knock at the door. They look at each other. Iona goes to open it. A bristling, proper, presbyterian, middle-aged stranger, a woman, is standing at the door. She looks snippy, and outraged.*

Mrs Henderson I am your neighbour, Mrs Henderson, from across the hall. I wish to complain about the terrible noise that's been coming out of this flat all night and all morning. What with all the shouting and music and arguing, myself and Mr Henderson haven't had a wink of sleep all night. You people are no better than you ought to be. Mark my words. I know what kind of people you are. You're the kind of people who'd have an answerphone and put a stupid message on it. Hostages to flimsy fashion. Think the world owes you a living. Comings and goings at all hours. All kinds and all sorts. Showing off. You ought to be ashamed of yourselves. I'm not finished with you yet. I kent your faither. And he was a jumped-up little upstart too. You needn't think you're anything special. I will be complaining to the council about you. You bring disgrace to the God-fearing decent name of Scotland.

She leaves abruptly, closing the door behind her.

Iona Oh my God. Our neighbour is a ghost from the gothic past. And the worst thing is, she really exists.

Kirsty Do you think that was Janice's mother?

Iona No. See, Kirsty, like I was trying to say, Janice Henderson – the Janice that was here a wee while ago – doesn't actually live across the hall.

Kirsty Oh. Right. Well, tell me her address. I'll get a taxi. I've plenty cash.

Iona Kirsty. Please. Listen. There is no Janice Henderson.

Kirsty No Janice Hend—?

Iona shakes her head.

But – but I saw her! With my own eyes! I spoke to her. She spoke back!

Iona (*indicating with her head, the wall, the audience*) No Janice Henderson across the hall. She came through the – *you* know.

Kirsty (*anguished*) She's from –? She's a –? She's one of them?

Iona I had to make something up. Because of Neil.

Kirsty Oh no. She went –?

Iona She did. She went.

Kirsty But – I can't go out there!

Iona I'm sorry, Kirsty.

Kirsty We can't go out there! Through there! We'd – I'd –

Iona Die.

Kirsty Oh no. Oh. Oh well. Oh, but . . . Okay. Yes.

Iona You know, I don't think she was really your type anyway. She was nice and everything. But a little material. She wanted a lot of money.

Kirsty She likes money, does she?

She begins to stuff the money all over the floor and in the rucksack into her clothes, into her pockets and down the front of her jumper.

Iona She could hardly be persuaded to talk about anything else.

Kirsty Do you think it's true what they say, that you can't take it with you?

Iona To be honest, Kirsty, she hardly noticed you. I don't think she even registered you were there. I don't know how much of a chance you'd stand with her.

Kirsty I'll persuade her. I'm very persuasive.

Iona And she was very coarse, really. She swore a lot. And who knows where she is now?

Kirsty (*positioning herself at the edge of the stage*) I'll find her. It'll be an adventure. I'll be a pioneer.

Iona And she told a lot of lies, for someone who demanded the truth so much.

Kirsty I'll be a visitor from another place. I'll be – an incomer. (*She is getting ready to jump.*)

Iona (*realising Kirsty is going to jump*) Kirsty!

Kirsty Here goes. Always give your whole self. All for love!

Iona What are you doing? Where are you going? You can't go –

Kirsty Be brave.

She waves to Iona. Gets ready. Somersaults herself off the stage, into the dark. She's gone.

Iona (*truly bereft, standing in the messy space of the stage*) What about the champagne? What about us being real sisters, you and me? What about the rest of the stories about the seer? There must be endless stories about the seer.

Short pause. She stands, useless. Enter Neil at the back with champagne and three glasses.

Neil Here we go. Where's Kirsty?

Iona Gone.

Neil Gone? How long will she be?

Iona Long enough.

Neil I'll put her glass here, then.

Iona She went like lightning. Just like she came.

Neil What shall we toast?

Iona The world made new, by different eyes.

Neil Eh? Okay then. Here's to it.

Iona Cheers.

Neil Cheers. To the eyes.

They drink.

Iona Here's to her.

Neil Wha's like her?

Iona Nobody. Nobody else. May all the worlds be kind to her. And here's to Janice. May she turn out to be everything Kirsty made of her. Or may the seer take his revenge.

Neil And here's to that English ghost, here's to her too

Iona May she rest in peace.

Neil Amen. (*He refills their glasses.*) We shouldn't be drinking this early in the morning, and before work, and everything.

Iona Here's to today. A holiday from work. Let's take the day off. We've earned it.

Neil Here's to it.

They sit down in their chairs, turn them towards each other.

You know, Iona. But when I first saw you. I thought. Who is this beautiful apparition passing before me?

Iona I know. I thought the same about you. I've known you all this time and I never knew you could sing!

Neil Well, I'd forgotten you could hear.

They sit together, in each other's arms.

Iona We could maybe go to bed.

Neil Since it's morning.

Iona Haven't said goodnight this late in the morning –

Neil – not since the old days.

Arms round each other, they're about to go through the back. But Iona turns, reluctant to go. She picks up Kirsty's glass, and drains it, looks out blindly at the wall, into the audience.

Neil What? What is it?

Iona What about them?

Neil (*timid again*) Aw, Iona, please, can we not just leave them be?

Iona I'd just like to . . .

Neil What?

Iona (*going to the karaoke machine*) Just something.

Iona plugs the machine in and switches it on. She chooses a song. She lets it start playing, Then she stands at the edge of the stage, blind, peering, listening hard. The words of whichever Scottish song she's chosen play up on the board. She's listening for the audience to start singing. With any luck, they will. (Even if they don't, it'll be poignant. But with Kirsty in the audience at least one voice will be there.)

Iona Can you hear?

Neil Hear what?

Iona Can you . . . ? Maybe it could be a bit louder . . .

Neil What about the neighbours?

Iona They can join in if they want. Can you hear voices? Singing?

Neil I can't. I told you. I can't hear a thing.

Iona Listen. Listen, can you hear that?

Neil No.

Iona Try harder.

Neil I can't hear a – oh. Wait. Was that –? That was –

Iona Did you hear? Did you hear something?

Neil I think . . . I think I can. I think I did. I think I can. I can.

Iona (*smiling*) Yes. I can too. I can hear her. I can hear them.

Iona and Neil join in the song. As the song comes to its end, they raise their glasses to the audience.

Blackout